Sequatchie County, Tennessee, County Court Minutes 1858-1874

Transcribed by:

Works Progress Administration

JANAWAY PUBLISHING, INC.
SANTA MARIA, CALIFORNIA

> *Notice*
>
> This book has been reproduced from carbon-copies of the original transcriptions of court records by the Works Progress Administration (WPA) in 1936. In many instances, the resulting text is light, the documents are physically flawed, and foxing (or discoloration) occurs. The pages of this reprint have been digitally enhanced and, where possible, the flaws eliminated in order to provide clarity of content and a pleasant reading experience. Furthermore, pages 21, 84, and 85 were all missing from the original book, as well as from the microfilm.

Sequatchie County, Tennessee, County Court Minutes 1858-1874

Originally transcribed by:

Works Progress Administration (WPA)
1936

Reprinted by:

Janaway Publishing, Inc.
732 Kelsey Ct.
Santa Maria, CA 93454
(805) 925-1038
www.JanawayGenealogy.com

2006, 2014

ISBN: 978-1-59641-029-9

Made in the United States of America

TENNESSEE

RECORDS OF SEQUATCHIE COUNTY

COUNTY COURT MINUTES
1858-1874

HISTORICAL RECORDS PROJECT
OFFICIAL PROJECT NO. 65-44-1493

COPIED UNDER WORKS PROGRESS ADMINISTRATION

MRS. JOHN TROTWOOD MOORE
STATE LIBRARIAN & ARCHIVIST, SPONSOR

ELIZABETH D. COPPEDGE
STATE DIRECTOR OF WOMEN'S & PROFESSIONAL PROJECTS

PENELOPE JOHNSON ALLEN
STATE SUPERVISOR

CAROLINE SMALL KELSO
SUPERVISOR THIRD DISTRICT

COPYISTS

MRS. GLADYS BLACK

JUNE 8, 1936

SEQUATCHIE COUNTY
COUNTY COURT MINUTES
VOL. 1
1858-1874

P-1   The County Court of Sequatchee met at the new meeting house near William Rankins, to organize and transact such other business as may come before it: according to an act passed by the Legislature of Tennessee, on the 9th day of December 1857.

Justices present - G. W. Cain, F. Deakins, Byram Heard, Aaron Smith and Thompson Hicks.

The Court organized by electing G, W, Cain, chairman, F. Deakins and Byram Heard Associate Justices.

The County Court then proceeded to appoint William Rankin Sheriff, and S. C. Stone, County Court Clerk, pro tem.

Ordered by the Court that A. B. Ewton, William Barker, J. L. Stone, A. R. Thurman and William D. Stewart beappointed to lay off and District the County of Sequatchee into Civil Districts and to designate the places of holding elections and to make return to the present term of the Court.

The Court then proceeded to the election of the Coroner. The candidate being George Rogers, he received five votes being the entire vote polled, and was declared elected for the term of two years.

The Court then proceeded to elect a Surveyor, the candidate being Burgess Taylor, he received five votes, being the entire vote polled, he was thereby declared duly and Constitutionally elected for the term of four years.

The Court then proceeded to the election of Ranger Frances McDonough being the only candidate received the entire vote polled being five and was declared elected for the term of two years.

The Court then proceeded to elect an Entry Taker, E. T. Sawyers received the entire vote polled and was elected for the term of four years.

P - 2   The Court then proceeded to elect a Tax Collector for the County of Sequatchee for the term of one year Howell Barker being the only candidate received the entire vote and was duly elected.

Ordered by the Court that a notice be served by the Sheriff of the County of Sequatchee upon the commissioners appointed by an act of the Legislature, to locate the County Site of Said County & C, to meet at Wm. Rankins, on the 25 instant, and attend to Said <u>buisiness</u>.

Ordered by the Court that Samuel W. Roberson, William D. Stewart, J. M. Anderson, Jesse Pickett, and William Barker, be appointed Commissioners according to act of the legislature to Superintend the laying off of the County, town, and directing the public buildings & C, and to perform all other required of them by said act.

Ordered by the Court that Madison Deakins be appointed guardian for Elizabeth McLain minor heir of Daniel McLain, Deceased.

The Commissioners appointed by the Court to district the County & C returned and made the following report,

The first Civil district of the County of Sequatchee Shall be composed of and bounded by the old district lines North and South, and on the East by the top of the mountain, and on the West by the river of Sequatchee, formally the Eastern portion of the tenth district of Bledsoe, The place of holding elections in the first district Shall be at the residence of John Welch.

The Second district Shall be on the opposite Side of the river, and bounded by the old district lines North and South, and on the west by the top of Cumberland Mountain and on the East by the Sequatchee river. The pace of holding elections for the Second district Shall be at the residence of Susan Smith.

P-3 The third district shall be composed of the Eastern half of the first Civil district formally of Marion County, bounded on the West by the Sequatchee river and on the East by the top of the mountain, the place of holding elections shall be at the house of James Richards.

The fourth district shall be composed of the Western half of the first Civil district formally of Marion Co. bounded on the East by the Sequatchee river, and on the West by the top of Cumberland Mountain. The place of holding eledtions Shall be at Wm. Rankins.

The fifth Civil district shall be composed of the Eastern half of the Second district formally of Marion County, bounded on the North and South by the old district lines, on the East by the top of Walden's Ridge and on the West by the Sequatchee river. The place of holding elections shall be at Clabom Gotts.

The Sixth district, Shall be on the West side of Sequatchee river, bounded on the North and South by the old district lines, on the East by the Sequatchee river, and on the West by the top of Cumberland Mountain, and the place of holding elections shall be at the old Medley place.

The Seventh district shall be composed of all the territory of the County of Sequatchee lying on the top of Walden's Ridge and shall hold their elections at the old Bunch place.

The eighth district Shall be composed of all the territory of Sequatchee County lying on the top of Cumberland mountain and shall hold their elections at the meeting house known by the name of Mt. Pleasant.

Commissioners: John L. Stone - A. B. Ewton - A. R. Thurman - Wm D. Stewart - William Barker.

P-4   The Court then adjourned until 9 o'clock tomorrow morning,
Geo. W. Cain, chm
Myrm Heard
F. Deakins.

Tuesday January 5th 1858.

The worshipful County Court of Sequatchee met pursuant to adjournment

Justices present, Geo W. Cain - Aaron Smith - Byram Heard - Thompson Hicks and F. Deakins.

S. C. Stone gave bond as required by law and took the oath of office as County Court Clerk of the County of Sequatchee pro tem.

William Rankin gave bond and took the oath of office as required by law, as Shiriff of the County of Sequatchee Tenn, pro tem.

George Rogers who was duly and Constitutionally elected Coroner for the County of Sequatchee appeared into open Court and gave bond with approved security, and took the oath of office required by law.

Burgess Taylor, who was elected Surveyor for the County of Sequatchee appeared into open Court and gave bond and took the oath of office as required by law.

Frances McDonough who was elected Ranker for the County of Sequatchee appeared into open Court gave bond with approved Security and took the oath of office as required by law.

E. T. Sawyers being duly and Constitutionally elected Entry Taker for the County of Sequatchee, appeared into open Court and gave his bond and took the oath of office required by law.

P-5   Ordered by the Court that B. B. Cannon be appointed Register for the County of Sequatchee, pro tem.

Ordered by the Court that Byram Heard, Thompson Hicks,

and Franklin Deakins are hereby appointed a committee to assess the taxes of Sequatchee County which assessment is in the words following, to wit, We the committee appointed by the County Court of Sequatchee County have this day proceeded to lay the taxes for said County for the year 1858, as follows, Forty cents on evry hundred dollars worth of real estate and personal property, and one dollar and twenty five cents on each and evry poll.

           Committee   (Thos. Hicks
                          (Byram Heard
                          (F. Deakins

Ordered by the Court that Olly Hatfield be appointed guardian for Franklin Harvey minor heir of William Harvey, Dec'd.

Ordered by the Court that the public roads in the County of Sequatchee be laid off into sections as follows, Beginning on the West side of Sequatchee river, on a first class road, from the County line of Sequatchee and Bledsoe to the Center of Big Brush Creek, James Ewton overseer and the same bounds of hands work under him as former overseer.

From the center of Big Brush Creek to the Center of Coop's Creek James Clemons, Overseer, the same bounds of hands work under him as former overseer.

From the center of Coop's Creek to the center of Stone's Creek M. M. Phelps, Overseer, to have the same bounds of hands work under him as former overseer.

From the center of Stone's Creek to the center of Thurman's Creek, William Deakins, overseer, the hands living on Mrs. Stone's place, Thos. Panky's place, James Deakin's place and Oliver Thurman's place work upon said road.

From the center of Thurman's Creek to the Southern County line, Harvey Hendrex, Overseer, all the hands from Thurman's Creek to the Southern County line, and from the mountain to Sequatchee river work on the said road, exept those who formally worked on the Cross road.

Beginning on the East side of Sequatchee river at the Northern County line to the center of Henson's Creek, Miligan Cordelle, Overseer, the same bounds of hands work under him as former ogerseer.

Ordered by the Court that the following Revenue Commissioners be appointed to take in the taxable property and free white polls for the year 1858.

District	1st	Aaron Smith	Dist.	5	John G. Barker
"	2	Byram Heard	"	6	Thompson Hicks
"	3	S. D. Thurman	"	7	Edwin Nunly
"	4	A. B. Ewton	"	8	Newton Clark

Ordered by the Court that the following persons be appointed a venire for the Circuit Court of Sequatchee County, to be holden on the fourth Monday and days following in May 1858.

Dist. 1st. Ephraim Welch - S. W. Roberson - A. R. Thurman & Aaron Smith
" 2. Jonathan Pope - Thos. Minton - Philip Hoots, & Byram Heard
" 3. S. D. Thurman - Wm. D. Stewart - John Cannon & Josiah Rogers
" 4. A. B. Ewton - Wm Heard - M. M. Phelps & Madison Deakins
" 5. Wm Barker - B. L. Bennett - Joshua Easterly & Henry Grayson
" 6. J. L. Stone - Jesse Pickett - Austin Hackworth
" 7. John Lewis
" 8. James Lockheart

P-6 Ordered by the Court that Jeremiah H. Hatfield wait upon the Circuit Court

Ordered by the Court that the Scholastic districts for the County of Sequatchee be composed of same bounds as the Civil districts of said county and numbered the same.

From the new Liberty meeting house to Thurman's branch David Brown, overseer, to have the same bounds of hands work under him as former overseer, except the Harvey's who live on William D. Stewart's place.

P-7 From S. D. Thurman's branch to the top of the hill above B. L. Bennett's, Joseph Easterly, overseer, to have the same bounds of hands as worked under former overseer.

From the top of the hill above B. L. Bennett's to the lane that leads to the river, then down said lane to the Sequatchee river, B. L. Bennett, overseer, to have all the hands on said Bennett's farm.

From the mouth of the lane at the Cross road to the Southern line of Sequatchee County, John Pickett, overseer, to have all the hands in said bounds to work under him except those formally attached to the Anderson mill road.

From near P. S. Rankins to Anderson's mill, James Barber, overseer, to have the same hands work on said road as work under former overseer.

Ordered by the Court that the County officer's bonds which were appointed and elected be spread of record.

Madison Deakins appeared into open Court and gave his bond as guardian of Elizabeth McClain minor heir of Daniel McClain, dec'd and took the oath required by law which was ordered to be spread of record.

Olly Hatfield appeared into open Court, and gave bond with approved security as guardian for Franklin Harvey minor heir of William Harvey dec'd which was ordered to be recorded.

The Court adjourned until tomorrow morning at 9 O'clock
Geo. W. Cain, Chm,
Byram Heard
F. Deakins

P-8   Wednesday, January term 1858.

Court met pursuant to adjournment Justices present, G. W. Cain, F. Deakins and Byram Heard,

Ordered by the Court that Aaron Smith be attached to the Mountain district it being the 7th Civil district of Sequatchee County.

Ordered by the Court that S. W. Roberson be appointed overseer of the Cross road from Thurman's bridge to the Valley road on the east side of Sequatchee river as a Second class road, to have all his own slave hands work on said road.

Ordered by the Court that S. W. Roberson be appointed overseer on a third class road, leading from where the Cross road intersects with Valley road to the top of the Mountain at Alex Gap, and have all his own hands work on said road.

Ordered by the Court that A. R. Thurman be appointed overseer on a Second class road, leading from Thurman's bridge to the Valley road on the West side of Sequatchee to have all the hands work on said road as worked under former overseer, Riley Andrew and David McWilliams.

Ordered by the Court that John Heard Jr. be appointed overseer on a Second Class road, beginning at Heard's old ford on Brush Creek, then running up Brush Creek to the mouth of the peach-tree lane, then up the lane to the main Valley road on the East side of the river, thus by the shop through the lane to the Henson road to have the same hands work on said road as worked under former overseer, also the two hands on John McWilliams place in the Bend.

Ordered by the Court that G. W. Cain Jr. be appointed overseer on a Second Class road from the center of Sequatchee river at Davis ford to the big road at Wm. Rankin's, then with the same to where the roads fork leading to McMinnville, then with said road to where William Heard's road intersects the same, to have all the hands on the farms of the old Bart Witson place J. S. Cain's farm on the West side of Sequatchee river Anderson Davis Wm Rankin G. W. Cain and J. H. Hatfield.

Ordered by the Court that James Lockheart be appointed overseer of Second class road from where Wm Heard's road intersects the old Hill turnpike road to the County line between the Counties of Sequatchee and Grundy, to have all the hands on the South side of Little Brush Creek in the eighth district.

Ordered by the Court that Marion Jones P-9 be appointed overseer on a Second class road, from the center of Sequatchee river at J. S. Cain's farm to the Valley road near New Liberty meeting house, then up said road to the Center of John Henson's Creek, also from the Valley road at Henson's to the foot of Walden's ridge to have same bounds of hands as former overseer, also the two Harvey's on W. D. Stewart's place.

Ordered by the Court that J. L. Stone be appointed overseer on a second class road from Ephraim Thurman's lane to the Sequatchee river, to have all the hands work on said road that live on the farms of Ephraim Thurman John Bennett, sen, J. L. Stone Wm M. Bennett, and Widows Brown & Barker formally

Ordered by the Court that Joseph Goleson be appointed overseer on a Third class road from near widow Hick's place on the Valley road to Thurman's turnpike road, near Widow Hick's place on Cumberland mountain to have the same bounds of hands as worked under former overseer.

Ordered by the Court that Sam W. Roberson's petition for a jury of view on a third class road, leading from Alex gap to the old turnpike road near John Lewis or E. S. Cards, and that the following persons be appointed a jury of view to locate and mark off said road, and report to the next term of this Court. Aaron Smith John Lewis, Washington Porter, Wm D Stewart, and Jason Harvey.

P-10 Ordered by the Court that Aaron Smith petition for a jury of view on a third class road, leading from Alex Gap in the directions of Jones Gap, on the opposite side of the mountain to the Hamilton County line, be granted, and that the following persons be appointed a jury of view to locate and mark off said road, Aaron Smith Wm D. Stewart Jason Harvey Washington Porter and John Lewis, And make return to the next term of this Court,

Ordered by the Court that William Rankin's petition for a Second class road, leading from the Spencer road to the old Hill turnpike, Beginning near Dick Hillis and terminating near Lewis Carlton's, be granted and the following persons be appointed a jury of view, to locate and work out said road, E. S. Owings, Newton Clark, James Blain, James Lockheart and John Russell, and make return to the next term of this Court.

Ordered by the Court that the following persons be appointed to hold an election on the first Saturday in March 1858, for the purpose of electing County and district officers,

Judges:
- Dist. 1st - Joel Wheeler, Ephraim Welch, A. R. Thurman
- "   2 - Jonathan Pope, Elij. Austin, Phil Hoots.
- "   3 - Geo. Stewart, Wm Brown, Sam'l Sparger
- "   4 - A. B. Ewton, McPhelps, Madison Deakins
- "   5 - Wm Barker, W. E. Kell, L. J. Hoodenpyle
- "   6 - J. L. Stone, E. Thurman, John Bennett
- "   7 - Jno. Lewis, Wash Porter, John Kell sr.
- "   8 - John Russell, Wm Williams, John Perry.

Clerks
- Dist. 1 - J. L. Hoge, John Welch
- "   2 - Jas. Billingsly, Thos. Minton
- "   3 - Wm D. Stewart, Jas. Richards
- "   4 - John Phelps, Wash Cain
- "   5 - B. L. Bennett, George Easterly
- "   6 - Oliver Thurman, Wm Bennett
- "   7 - Burgess Taylor, Jason Harvey
- "   8 - E. S. Owings, Newton Clark

Ordered by the Court that William D. Stewart A. Smith and John Lewis be appointed to lay off the Seventh Civil district into three Scholastic districts, and report to the next term of this Court.

B. B. Cannon who was appointed by the County Court of Sequatchee register, pro.tem, appeared into open Court and gave his bond with approved security and took the oath of office as required by law.

P-11   The Court then adjourned until tomorrow morning at 9 o'clock   G. W. Cain Chm. Byram Heard, F. Deakins.

Thursday, January 7th 1858

Quorum Court met pursuant to adjournment. Esqrs Cain, Heard and Deakins present.

Ordered by the Court that John H. Rogers and William D. Stewart be appointed commissioners on the Poe turnpike road for the County of Sequatchee.

Ordered by the Court that Joshua Easterly and Wm. Barker be appointed Commissioners on the Anderson turnpike road for the County of Sequatchee

Ordered by the Court that James W. Hatfield be appointed overseer on the public road leading from the Valley road on the East side of Sequatchee river, by Hatfield's bridge to the Valley road on the West side of Said river, and that he have George Stewart's hands F. J. Johnson, Nimrod Kell, James W. Hatfield Isaac Williams and John B. Hatfield work on said road.

Ordered by the Court that Madison Deakins and Joseph Goleston be appointed Commissioners on the Thurman turnpike for the County of Sequatchee

Ordered by the Court that a charter for a toll bridge be granted to James W. Hatfield, across Sequatchee river in the County of Sequatchee, and that said bridge be considered a lawful bridge as it now stands in regard to its width.

Ordered by the Court that a notice be served upon the Commissioners appointed by the County Court of Sequatchee at its January term 1858, to lay off the County town direct the public building & C, to appear at the next term of this Court and give bond and soforth, as required by an act of the Legislature.

P-12 Ordered by the Court that George K. Larrimore be attached to the fourth Civil district of Sequatchee County. Ordered by the Court that B. B. Cannon's petition for a jury of view to change a Second class road leading from the old ford on Sequatchee river at Davis farm to intersect the old road above the slue on J. X. Cain's place, be granted, and that the following persons be appointed a jury of view to locate and mark of said road
John Cannon, Wm. D. Stewart, Wm Rogers Joseph Davis and James Jones.

James W. Hatfield appeared into open Court and gave bond with approved sedurity, for the performance of his duties as keeper of a toll bridge,

Ordered by the Court that notice be served upon the Revenue Commissioners appointed by the County Court of Sequatchee, to appear at the next term of this Court to receive instructions in regard to their duty as revenue Commissioners,

Court adjourned until Court in Course
    George W. Cain,
    Byram Heard,) Associate
    F. Deakins) Justices

Dunlap, February 1st 1858

Quorum Court met pursuant to adjournment Justices on the bench, Cain, Heard & Deakins The Commissioners appointed to lay off the Seventh Scholastic district, appeared, into Court and made the following report,

We the Commissioners being duly sworn have agreed to let the old lines of the Scholastic districts stand as they were originally

    Com,
    Wm D. Stewart
    John Lewis
    Aaron Smith

P-13 Jury of view report,

We the undersigned after being duly sworn have proceeded to view and mark out a third class road described in the within order, This 21st Jany, 1858

    Washington Porter Aaron Smith
    Jason Harvey Wm D. Stewart
    S. W. Roberson John Lewis

Report of jury of view,

We the undersigned jury of view after being duly sworn proceeded to view and mark a third class road from Alex Gap to intersect the Poe road near the Bunch place agreeably to the Contents of the within order, January 21st 1858,

    John Lewis Wm D. Stewart
    Jason Harvey S. W. Roberson
    Aaron Smith C. W. Coleman

Jury of view report,

We the undersigned jury of view have proceeded to view and mark out a road leading from Dixon Hillis to intersect the Hill turnpike road near John Rickett's, to the Grundy County line, Said Rickett agreeing to cut out the remainder, being near a quarter of a mile in length, Jany 27th 1858,

    E. S. Owings James Lockheart
    James Blair Lewis W. Carlton

Jury of view report

We the undersinged jury of view prodeeds to lay off and mark out and change the road from Davis fork leading up the river on said Davis side and Crossing it above the slue on John Cain's farm, Jany 15th 1858,

        William D. Stewart
    James Jones Joseph Davis
    B. B. Cannon William Rogers

State of Tennessee) Feb. term 1858
Sequatchee County) Ordered by the Court that Miligan Cordle be appointed overseer on a Second class road, leading from the Center of Henson's Creek to the line between the same bounds of hands as worked under former overseer except William Hixon

P-14
State of Tennessee) February term 1858
Sequatchee County) Ordered by the Court that Aaron Smith be appointed overseer on a Second class road, from the County line of Bledsoe and Sequatchee Counties, to S. W. Roberson's and the widow Hixon's line, to have all the hands in said bounds.

 Ordered by the Court that all persons south of Woodcock's Creek round to the Bennett place be attached to the Sixth Civil district of Sequatchee County.

 Ordered by the Court that John Dill be attached to the Second Civil district of Sequatchee County.

Ordered by the Court that Ake Craig be appointed overseer on a third class road leading from near Jesse Pickett's shop across the ridge to the old Laughby ford, to have all the hands on Benj. Allen's farm to work on said road.

Ordered by the Court that John Heard Jr. be appointed overseer on a third class road, Beginning at Heard's old ford and running up Brush Creek on the East side to the shallow ford, then around A. B. Ewtons field as the old road now runs to intersect the main Stage road where the Savage road intersects said road, to have the same bounds of hands as worked under former overseer.

Ordered by the Court that a mill road be changed leading to Hatfield's mill, so as to run on the line between Hatfield's and Deakins until it intersects the old mill road according to agreement between said parties.

George Rogers who was elected Coroner by the County Court of Sequatchee offered his resignation which was accepted.

Ordered by the Court that Jonathan Hatfield be appointed Coroner in lieu of George Rogers, resigned.

P-15 Ordered by the Court that the appointment of Commissioners appointed by the County Court to superintend the town of Dunlap was illegal and is hereby revoked and others appointed in their places,

Ordered by the Court that Thomas Davis be appointed overseer on a third class road from Alex Gap to the Hamilton County line, towards Hugh's gap, The following are the bounds of hands to work on said road From Alex gap with the Bledsoe County line to the Hamilton line then with it to Soddy Creek thus up it ot the top of the mountain.

Ordered by the Court that Jason Harvey be appointed overseer on a third class road from Alex Gap to the Center of Board Camp Creek above the saw mill, to have the following bounds of hands, From the mill to the top of the mountain so as to include E. Newby then to Davis bounds.

Ordered by the Court that John Lewis be appointed overseer on a third class road from the center of Board Camp Creek above the sawmill to the Poe turnpike road near John Lewis, to have the following bounds of hands, from the mill to the top of the mountain near E. Newby's leaving him out, then down the mountain to Cooper's Creek then down it to the County line.

Ordered by the Court that Wm D. Stewart be appointed a Commissioner to examine and license teachers for the free schools of Sequatchee County.

The Court then adjourned until one hour.

Court met pursuant to adjournment, The Commissioners appointed by the Legislature to locate the County Cite for Sequatchee County appeared into open Court and made the following report,

P-16 We the Commissioners Byram Heard, John L. Stone F. Deakins John Pickett B. L. Bennett John H. Rogers and Sam'l W. Roberson commissioners appointed by the Legislature to locate a County site for the County of Sequatchee, after being duly summons and sworn, proceeded upon the duties assigned us by the Legislature and after determining upon the Center of the County, sufficiently near to enable us to act, proceeded to examine various situations and upon consultation and taking the vote of our body we determined to locate the County site upon the farm of Wm Rankin forty acres for said location and herewith present his bond for title, This 1st Feb, 1858

   Sam'l W. Roberson   Byram Heard
   Secty.   Chairman

Ordered by the Court that the following commissioners be appointed to superintend the laying off of the town of Dunlap directing the public buildings & C, Sam'l W. Roberson S. C. Stone William Phelps, Edwin Newby and William Rankin,

Ordered by the Court that James I. Rogers be appointed overseer on a third class road from the end of Gotts and Anderson's lane to Anderson's mill, to have all the hands on Anderson's farm except Mauzer Ellis.

Ordered by the Court that James I. Rogers be appointed overseer on a second class road from the top of the hill above Clabe Gotts to Anderson's shop to have all the hands on Anderson's farm exdept Mauzer Ellis.

The Court then adjourned until tomorrow morning at 9 o'clock
       George W. Cain
        Chairman
      Byram Heard &
      Franklin Deakins
       Associate Justices

P117   Dunlap February 2nd 1858,

Quorem Court met pursuant to adjournment Jonathan Hatfield who was appointed Coroner by the County Court of Sequatchee appeared into open Court and gave his bond which was approved, and took the oath of office as required by law.

Ordered by the Court that William Rankin's petition for a jury of view be granted to change the public road from Coop's Creek so as to run with the Main Street of Dunlap up to the first mile post

Jury of view, G. W. Cain A B Ewton George Walker William

Phelps & Byram Heard.

Ordered by the Court that James Blain be appointed overseer on a Second class road from the County line of Sequatchee and Van Buren to the County line of Grundy to have all the hands North of James Lockhearts bounds of hands.

Ordered by the Court that Notice be Served upon the Commissioners appointed by the County Court at its Feb. term 1858, to lay off the town of Dunlap & C to appear at the present time of this Court and give their bond as required by law,

The Court adjourned for one hour and a half.

Court met pursuant to adjournment.

The Commissioners appointed at the present time of this Court, to superintend the laying off of the town of Dunlap & C, appeared into Court and gave their bond as required by act of the Genral Assembly, and took the oath of office required by law.

The Court then adjourned until tomorrow morning at 11 o'clock
                          G. W. Cain, Chm,
                          Byram Heard
                          F. Deakins

P-18 Quorem Court met pursuant to adjournment. Byram Heard Chairman of the board of commissioners appointed by an act of the legislature to locate the County site of Sequatchee & C, made a transfer upon the bond of William Rankin for title to land for said location, to the Commissioners appointed by the County to lay off said site & C in the following words and figures to wit,

State of Tennessee)   I, Byram Heard chairman of the board
Sequatchee County)   of commissioners appointed by an act of the Legislature to locate the town of Dunlap & C, do hereby transfer the bond of Wm Rankin for title, to the Commissioners appointed by the County Court for said County, to wit, Sam'l W. Roberson S. C. Stone, Wm Phelps Edwin Newby and William Rankin, This 3rd Feb 1858,   Byram Heard
                                        Chm, of the board of com,

There being nofurther buisness the Court adjourned until Court in Course,
                                Geo. W. Cain
                                    Chairman
                                Byram Heard
                                Franklin Deakins.

Dunlap Tenn, Monday April 5th 1858

The County Court of Sequatchee County and state of Tenne-

14.

ssee met this the 5th day of April 1858 pursuant to adjournment. Justices present G. W. Cain F Deakins Aaron Smith and Byram Heard.

Ordered by the Court that the former order attaching Aaron Smith to the South Civil district be recinded

It is ordered by the Court that patrolls be appointed in the 3rd Civil district in the County of Sequatchee William Rogers Capt. and J. M. Richards & Malcolm Johnson.

P-19   Order that patrolls be appointed in the first district Aaron Smith, Miligan Cordle & J. L. Hoge

Ordered by the Court that Alfred King be appointed Capt. of patroll company for the fourth district and also M. M. Phelps and Bird Harmon.

Ordered by the Court that patrolls be appointed in the fifth district, P. F. Rankin Capt. George Easterly and Mauzer Ellis.

Ordered by the Court that patrolls be appointed in the sixth Civil district of Sequatchee County Thos. Pankey, Capt. Jesse Pickett & James Kicks

Ordered by the Court that George Walker be appointed administrator of Philip A Walker dec'd.

Ordered by the Court that Joseph Davis be appointed guardian for the minor heirs of his wife Betsy Ann Davis <u>formally</u> Betsy Ann Heard, heir of john Heard deceased.

Ordered by the Court that the following Commissioners be appointed to lay off to the widow of Philip A. Walker her portion of the estate of Said Walker dec'd. A. B. Ewton Wm B. Elliott and John Teaters.

Ordered by the Court that the 9th Civil district be formed in the County of Sequatchee Beginning at the top of Cumberland mountain and running up Little Brush Creek to the new marked road from D. Hillis to the Hill road then to the James Cagle place includeing James B. Smith in Said district, there with the Grundy County line Southwardly to near the Brewer place and the place of holding elections to be at A. J. Tate's.

Ordered by the Court that the <u>Shiriff</u> open and hold an election in all the Civill districts in the County of Sequatchee on the 17th day of April 1858, for the purpose of electing Justices of the peace and Constables.

P-20   Ordered by the Court that Jesse Savage, A. J. Tate and James B. Smith, be appointed Judges to hold an election in the 9th district on the 17th day of April 1858, for the purpose of electing district officers.

Ordered by the Court that the revenue commissioners met at William Rankin's on the last Saturday in April instant, to equalize their tax lists.

Ordered by the Court that John C. Rickett be appointed revenue Com. for the 9th Civil district for the year 1858.

Ordered by the Court that the place of holding elections in the eighth Civil district be changed from Mt. Pleasant to the Woodley place.

Ordered by the Court that William Smith be appointed overseer on a second class road from the old Marion County line to Peyton Christians to have the same bounds of hands as worked on Said portion of the road _formally_ except John Clemons who is to work under Christian.

Ordered by the Court that William O'Neal be appointed overseer on a second class road from Peyton Christians to the Warren County line, to have the same bounds of hands as worked under former overseer.

Ordered by the Court that the petition of E. S. Owings for a jury of view be granted, to locate a road from the top of the hill near E. S. Owings to the Van Buren County line to intersect the Myres road, James Blain Newton Clark and E. S. Owings Jury of View

Ordered by the Court that Trustee be appointed to fill the vacancy occasioned by not electing a Trustee at the regular time for such elections, the Court then appointed George Walker Trustee, pro tem, who gave bond with approved Security as required by law, and took the oath of office.

P-21 Howell Barker who was elected Tax Collector for the year 1858, at the January term of the County Court for Sequatchee County, appeared into open Court and gave his bonds with approved security as required by law.

Ordered by the Court that the venire which was appointed, for the Circuit Court to be holden on the fourth Monday and days following in May, be revived and Constituted a venire for the Circuit Court to be held on the   Monday and days following in June 1858, by the Judges of the sixteenth Judicial Circuit.

Ordered by the Court that the Judges and Clerks who were appointed by the County Court at its Jany term 1858 to hold an election for County and district officers, on the first Saturday in March 1858, are hereby Constituted Judges and Clerks to holden election on the 17th day of April 1858 for Justices of the peace and Constables,

Report of jury of view,

We the undersigned jury of view have proceeded to view and mark a first class road from Coop's Creek so as to intersect the Main Street of Dunlap and to intersect the main road near the first mile post.
George W. Cain William Rankin & A. B. Ewton

Ordered by the Court that Granville Hatfield have the children of Martha Hatfield bound to him, to wit, Martha Patience, James and John Hatfield, For which said Granville Hatfield binds himself to give to each one of the boys six months schooling besides sending them to the free schools, and at the age of twenty one he is to give them a horse bridle saddle and blanket worth seventy five dollars and two suits of good clothes, and to the girl the same as the boys at the age of eighteen. The ages of the children bound to Granville Hatfeild are as follows, Martha Patience about eight or nine years old, Hames about five or six years old, John three or four years old.

P-22 The Court then adjourned until tomorrow morning at
9 O'clock
      George W. Cain, Chairman
      Byram Heard
      F. Deakins.

Tuesday April 6th 1858

The Court met pursuant to adjournment, Justices present G. W. Cain F. Deakins and Byram Heard.

Ordered by the Court that the order made yesterday establishing patrolls for various districts in the County be recinded.

Ordered by the Court that the County tax upon stud horses and jacks, be the season price of such stud or jack.

Ordered by the Court that the appointment of George Walker as administrator of the estate of P. A. Walker as administrator of P. A. Walker dec'd be and the same is hereby recinded.

There being no further buisiness the Court then adjourned until Court in Course
      George W. Cain Chm
      Byram Heard,
      F. Deakins,

Dunlap Tenn, May 3rd 1858,

Quorum Court met on this the 3rd day 1858 at the new meeting house near William Rankin's to transact such buisiness as may come before it, Justices present G. W. Cain, F. Deakins Aaron Smith Byram Heard and Thos. Hicks.

Ordered by the Court that the Seventh Scholastic district be formed out of all the territory on Walden's Ridge that formally belonged to the first Civil district of Marion County.

Ordered by the Court that the tenth Scholastic district

be formed out of all the territory on Walden's P-23 ridge that formally belonged to the tenth Civil district of Bledsoe County.

Ordered by the Court that the eleventh Scholastic district be formed out of all the territory on Walden's ridge that formally belonged to the second Civil district of Marion County.

Ordered by the Court that a third class road be established in the County of Sequatchee from near A. J. Tate's on the old hill road to the Grundy County line in the direction of the Thurman turnpike road, Jesse Savage overseer, Dalphin Night and J. W. Tate work on said road,

The Court having no further buisiness to transact adjourned until Court in Course,
                          George W. Cain, Chairman
                          Byram Heard
                          F. Deakins.

Dunlap Tenn, Monday, June 7th 1858,

Quorum Court met pursuant to adjournment, Present on the bench, G. W. Cain, F. Deakins Byram Heard and Aaron Smith,

It is ordered by the Court that Olly Hatfield guardian for Franklin Harvey minor heir of William Harvey dec'd be authorized to collect any debts that were owing to said Harvey dec'd.

Ordered by the Court that S. W. Roberson and Ephraim Welch be appointed Commissioners to assess the value of John McWilliams real estate in the first district, and report to the next quarterly Court.

It appearing to the Court that John F. Kennon has died intestate, it is ordered that Wm. B. Elliott and Jeremiah Walker be appointed administrators of the estate of said Kennon dec'd. and that letters testementary issue to them, There being no further buisiness the Court adj. until Court in Course,
                          G. W. Cain, Chm.
                          B. Heard
                          F. Deakins

P-24 The worshipful County Court for the County of Sequatchee met pursuant to adjournment. Present on the bench, Esqrs G. W. Cain, F. Deakins Byram Heard Aaron Smith and Thompson Hicks.

The Justices who were elected on the 17th day of April 1858, except S. D. Thurman Edwin Newby and John Odum, came forward and took the oath required by law and took their seats, to wit, G. W. Nichols Joel B. Austin M. B. Narrimore Wm B. Elliott John C. Lockhart Wm E. Kell J. W. Morrison I. C.

Rickett A. H. Lockhart, E. S. Owings and I. N. Clark all of whom gave bond under the small offence law, except G. W. Nichols Edwin Newby John Odum & S. D. Thurman

The Court then proceeded to lay a County tax upon privaleges.

Merchant's license, ¼ per.cent say twenty five cents on the hundred worth at invoice cost where purchased, County tax on deeds at registration fifteen cents on the hundred acres.

Grocery privaleges, Twenty five Dollars Circus Shares fifty dollars for each day & night concerts, Five Dollars for each day & night

For hawking and peddling, for vehicle $30 for horse $20 for footman $10.

The vote being taken on an allowance to William Rankin for eighty four dollars and twenty five cents, for books furnished the County Court of Sequatchee, and also a County Seal. Those who voted in the affirmation were Aaron Smith G. W. Nichols, Byram Heard M. B. Narrimore G. W. Cain F. Deakins Wm B. Elliott, Wm E. Kell J. C. Lockheart, J. M. Morrison Thos. Hicks E. S. Owings I. N. Clark, A.H. Lockhart and J. C. Rickett,

Those in the negative (none)

It is therefore ordered by the Court that the Trustee pay the same P-25 out of the monies in his hands not otherwise appropriated and that Certificate Issue.

Ordered by the Court that the minutes of this Court be transcribed into the new minute book marked letter A by S. C. Stone the Clerk of the County Court,

Ordered by the Court that B. B. Cannon, register, be required to tranxcribe the deeds & C into the new book marked letter A which has been purchased for that purpose.

The vote of the Court being taken on an allowance of four dollars to each revenue Commissioner for taking down the taxable property in their respective districts, Those who voted in the affirmation were, A. Smith G. W. Nichols Byram Heard M. B. Narrimore G. W. Cain F. Deakins Wm B. Elliott Wm E. Kell J. C. Lockhart J. M. Morrison Thompson Hicks E. W. Owings I. N. Clark A. H. Lockheart and J. C. Rickett, Negative, none.

It is therefore ordered by the Court that the Trustee pay the same out of any county monies not otherwise appropriated, and that Certificate issue.

Ordered by the Court that Wm Williams be appointed overseer on a third class road the old Savage road from the main Valley road near A. B. Ewton's to a point about one half mile beyond Mt. Pleasant meeting house, and that he have all the hands between the two brush creeks from the top of the mountain to work on said road. (Iss'd)

Aaron Smith who was appointed overseer on a second class road on the East side of Sequatchee river, returns his order which is accepted by the Court and it is ordered that said portion of the road be attached to Miligan Codle's order and that he work it with the same boundary of hands which his and Said A. Smiths included.(Iss'd)

It is ordered by the Court that the hands on Jesse Pickett's home place work on a cross road leading from near his shop across the ridge to the old Laughby ford on Sequatchee river. P-26 The Commissioners appointed at the last term of the Court to assess the valuation of John McWilliams real estate, brought in their report and assess the property at five thousand seven hundred and fifty dollars and it is ordered the same be taxed only to said amount. (Iss'd)

Elias Clemons produced in open Court the scalp of one Wild Cat, which he prooved to the Satisfaction of the Court had been killed by him in the bounds of Sequatchee County. It is therefore ordered by the Court Certificate issue to him. (Iss'd)

William D. Stewart prooved in open Court, five of the acting Justices of the peace being present, the scalp of one wolf which he prooved to the Satisfaction of the Court was killed by him in the bounds of Sequatchee County, and that the same was over four months old. It is therefore ordered by the Court that the Treasurer of the State of Tennessee pay said William D. Stewart six dollars out of any monies in his hands not otherwise appropriated and that Certificate issue. (Iss'd)

Ordered by the Court that Jonathan Pope George W. Cain William Rankin, M.B. Narrimore and William B. Elliott be appointed Trustees of the Rankin Academy in the County of Sequatchee, to have all the powers rights and privaliges of the other Trustees of County Academies in the State of Tennessee.

It appearing to the Satisfaction of the Court that there is in the hands of Sam M. C. Brown former turstee of Marion County, about the sum of one hundred and forty dollars belonging to the old common School districts of said Marion County now included within the bounds of Sequatchee County, and it further appearing to the satisfaction of the Court that the Said citizens included in the bounds of said County, Are intitled to draw and apply said monies.

It is therefore ordered by the Court that the said former Trustee of Marion County pay over to George Walker trustee of Sequatchee County, P-27 all monies in his hands properly belonging to or for the use of Common Schools in said Sequatchee County, and that the Truste of said County apply said monies for the use of Common schools to those by law entitled to receive the same.

Wm B. Elliott and Jeremiah Walker administrators of the estate of John F. Kennon dec'd returned into open Court an inventory and account of sales of the estate of said decedent which is ordered to be recorded.

Sam'l W. Roberson S. C. Stone Edwin Newby William Phelps & Wm Rankin Com. appointed by this Court in pursuance of law, to lay out the town of Dunlap in the County of Sequatchee and superentend the erection of a Court house and jail for said County etc & C made the following report.

To the worshipful County Court of Sequatchee County at July term 1858, The following Com. appointed by the County Court of Sequatchee County, to wit, William Rankin William Phelps Edwin Newby S. C. Stone & Sam'l W. Roberson to lay off and sell the lots in the town of Dunlap, organized by appointing William Rankin president and Sam'l W. Roberson secretary and treasurer of said town into sixth eight lot which the assistance of B Taylor County surveyor and Thad Sims & T, Pankey, chain carriers, a plot of which is herewith filed, and they further designate lot no1 62 in said plan of the town for the erection of a County Jail, and lot 58 for the Presbyterean and Methodist denominations, for the erection of a church or churches, and lot No. 49 for the Baptist, to wit, the old Baptist and the Missionary Baptist.

And William Rankin proposing to give or donate to the Trustees of Rankin Academy a lot of ground near the town for the purpose of erecting an Academy thereon, we accept the same.

The sale of said lots, we advertised and sold in part on the 26th April 1858, the following lots to persons as follows to wit,

No. Lots-	Persons-	Valuation
1 2 3 4 & 5	William Rankin	$435 50/100
6	Sam'l W. Roberson	200.
7	B. B. Cannon	126.
8	J. M. Richards	95.
9 & 10	Edwin Newby	190.
11 & 12	William Hatfield	131.
14	J. H. Hatfield	52.
15	S. H. Colms	64.
16	F. Deakins	50.
17	Geo. W. Cain	40.
18	J. Hixon	30.
20, 21 & 25	J. F. Kennon	217.
30	Jonathan Hatfield	130.
50	James Mansfield	83.

PAGE 21 MISSING FROM MICROFILM AND FILE

And that George W. Heard attend as Constable at said Court.

    Court then adjourned until tomorrow morning at 8 O'clock
                            George W. Cain, Chm.
                            Byram H. Heard
                            F. Deakins
                            J. M. Morrison

Tuesday July 6th 1858,

    Court met at the House assigned by law for holding Courts for Sequatchee County pursuant to adjournment. P-30 Present on the bench the worshipful George W. Cain, Byram Heard Wm B. Elliott John C. Lockheart, M. B. Narrimore Franklin Deakins J. M. Morrison and A. H. Lockhart, Esqrs, Justices & C John Odum who was duly and Constitutionally elected a justice of the peace in the bounds of the Seventh Civil district of Sequatchee County, on the 17th day of April 1858 for the ensuing Constitutional term - appeared in open Court proceeded his Commission and took all the necessary oaths for his qualifications gave bond as required by law and took his seat upon the bench.

    Whereas it is represented to this Court that George Rogers late of Sequatchee County has departed this life intestate and the Court being satisfied as to the rights of James W. Hatfield to the administration.

    It is therefore ordered by the Court that he be appointed administrator of all and Singular the goods chattels rights and Credits of said George Rogers and thereupon said Hatfield entered into bond in the final sum of Eight hundred dollars with Josiah Rogerxs his Security which bond is approved by the Court, and said Hatfield thereupon was duly qualified as administrator issue to him.

    Ordered by the Court that Jonathan Hatfield, George Stewart & F. J. Johnson be appointed Com. to lay off and set apart an allowance of one years provisions for the support of Susan Rogers widow of George Rogers dec'd and her family one year from the death of her husband and that they report to next Court. (Iss'd)

    Ordered by the Court that the <u>Shiriff</u> open and hold elections at the election grounds in the 1st & 8th Civil districts in Sequatchee County, after giving legal notice of the time of holding said elections, for the purpose of electing one Constable in each of said districts and report to next Court. (Iss'd)

P-31 Ordered by the Court that Levi Hackworth be appointed overseer on a public road in the place of Harvey Hendrix, that the same bounds of hands work under him that were bound to work under former overseer, said road being a first class road.

  Court adjourned until Court in Course.
        George W. Cain, Chairman
        F. Deakins
        Byram Heard

  Dunlap, Tenn, Monday 2nd Aug, 1858.

  County Court met pursuant, to adjournment present on the bench Aaron Smith F. Deakins Byram Heard M. B. Narrimore Wm B. Elliott, A. H. Lockhart J. C. Lockhart Wm E. Kell.

  G. W. Cain, Chairman of this Court being absent it is ordered that Aaron Smith be appointed Chairman, pro tem.

  L. D. Thurman who was elected justice of the peace on the 17th day of April 1858, for the third district of Sequatchee County, then appeared into open Court and gave bond under the Small offence law and took the oaths required by law, and took his seat upon the bench.

  George Stewart Jonathan Hatfield and F. J. Johnson who were appointed Commissioners to lay off one years provisions to the widow of George Rogers dec'd made the following report, which is ordered to be recorded.

  Pursuant to an appointment by the County Court of Sequatchee County Jonathan Hatfield George Stewart and F. J. Johnson met and laid off the years provisions for Susan Rogers widow of George Rogers late of said County dec'd the following is the allowance made to her by them.
  All the crop of Corn and wheat
  seven head of hogs for meat.
P-32 Ten head of Stock hogs
  Fifteen dollars in cash to be paid out of the first money collected from the proceeds of the Sale of the proceeds of the Sale of the property belonging to the estate.
  All the Bacon on hand
  All the old Corn on hand
  All the Soap Salt and fowls on hand
    George Stewart   James W. Hatfield
    Jonathan Hatfield   Administrator.
    F. J. Johnson

  Cornet Hatfield produced in open Court the scalp of one Wild cat which he prooved to the Satisfaction of the Court was killed by him within the bounds of Sequatchee County.

  It is therefore ordered by the Court that Certificate issue to him.

  The Coroner for the County of Sequatchee presented to the Court the verdict of a jury of inquest which was held upon the body of Philip A. Walker which was ordered to be recorded

Inquisition of Suidide.

We, being duly impanneled sworn and charged by the Coroner of the County of Sequatchee, State of Tenn, as a jury of inquest to enquire how when and in what manner Philip A. Walker on the 27th day of February 1858, in the County of Sequatchee and State aforesaid did unlawfully and voluntarily kill himself, by shooting himself with a rifle gun, against the peace and dignity of the State,

Given and rendered by us, This 27th Feb. 1858

         Jonathan Pope, Foreman
         B. B. Cannon,
   Jonathan Hatfield   Caswell Ewton
    Coroner of Said County John Seatins
         Philip Hoots
         Ausberry Bevert
         William McGlothlin
         Jas. H. Cannon
   James Ewton   John Clemons
   G. W. Smith,   John Cannon

P-33   Edwin Newby who was elected Justice of the peace for the Seventh Civil district of Sequatchee County State of Tennessee on the 17th day of April 1858, appeared into open Court took the oaths of office required by law and gave bond under the small offence law, and took his seat upon the bench.

  B. J. Bailey Constable elected on the 17th day of April 1858 for the fifth Civil district of Sequatchee County appeared into open Court, took the oaths required by law and gave his bonds which was approved by the Court.

  It appearing to the Satisfaction of the Court that there is in the hands of the Trustee of Grundy County seventy four dollars ninety three and three fourths cents common school monies due the seventh Scholastic district, formally of Grundy County, for the year 1858, and also the amount due that portion of the territory of said County which was attached to Sequatchee County by the last Legislature for the year 1858. It is thereupon ordered by the Court that the Trustee of Grundy County pay the same over to George Walker Trustee of Sequatchee County Tenn. (Iss'd)

  Ordered by the Court that William B Elliott be appointed to make a book case for the clerk of the County Court to keep the records & C safely and also to make a temporary jury romm in the house where the Courts are now held.

  J. W. Tate Constable elected on the 17th April 1858, for the 9th Civil district of Sequatchee County appeared into Court and took the oaths and gave bonds required by law.

  Court adjourned until court in Course
       Aaron Smith Chm

Byram Heard
F. Deakins

P-34   Dunlap, Monday Septr 6th 1858.

Quorem Court met pursuant to adjournment, present on the bench G. W. Cain Aaron Smith, I. M. Morrison E. S. Owings I. N. Clark M. B. Narrimore Wm E. Kell, E. Newby Byram Heard, F. Deakins

It appearing to the Satisfaction of the Court that there is common School moneys belonging to the County of Sequatchee in the hands of the Trustee of Bledsoe County,

It is therefore ordered by the Court that the Trustee of Sequatchee County apply to the Trustee of Bledsoe Co. for the amount due said fractional part of Sequatchee County, formally of Bledsoe.

It appearing to the Satisfaction of the Court that there is in the hands of the Trustee of Marion County common School moneys belonging to Sequatchee County.

It is thereupon ordered by the Court that the Trustee of Sequatchee County apply to the Trustee of Marion County for the amt. due the fractional part of Sequatchee County formally of Marion.

Bird Clark, who was elected Constable for the 9th Civil district of Sequatchee County appeared into open Court gave the bonds required by law and took the necessary oaths for his qualification the former order of Court for a new election being recinded.

James W. Hatfield returned into open Court an inventory of the personal property of George Rogers dec'd together with a list of the Sales of said property sworn to in open Court.

Ordered by the Court that Edward Picket be appointed overseer on a first class road from the Centre of Thurman's Creek to the Southern County line on the West side of Sequatchee river, and that he have all the hands on the following farms work on said road John Griffith's John Picket, John A. Pickets on the west side of Sequatchee river Davis Hoodenpyle Jesse Picketts farm on the west side of the same river Isaac Hicks Wisow Hicks, Widow   P-35   Hendrex and Thompson Hicks.

It is ordered by the Court that Peyton Christian John Russell and James Blain be appointed Commissioners to locate a suitable site for erection of a School house in the eighth district of Sequatchee County, and that they meet on the 9th September for that purpose.

George W. Heard Constable elect for the fourth Civil district of Sequatchee County tenders his resignation to the

Court which is accepted.

It is therefore ordered by the Court that the <u>Shiriff</u> open and hold an election in said district for Constable to fill the vacancy occasioned by the resignation of G. W. Heard.

Court adjourned until Court in Course
George W. Cain, Chm.
Byram Heard
F. Deakins

Dunlap Oct 4th 1858.

Court met pursuant to adjournment Present on the bench G. W. Cain Byram Heard A Smith G. W. Nichols J. B. Austin Wm B. Elliott M. B. Narrimore S. D. Thurman Wm E. Kell J. C. Lockhart Edwin Newby E. S. Owings I. N. Clark

I. N. Clark was appointed by the Court to take charge of John Cagle as a pauper until the next term of the Quarterly Court.

The vote of the Court being taken on an allowance of two dollars & ninety cents to I. N. Clark for necessaries furnished John Cagle a pauper by said Clark. Those who voted in the affirmative were, G. W. Cain Wm B. Elliott E. S. Owings Byram Heard Edwin Newby J. C. Lockhart Wm E. Kell M. B. Narrimore S. D. Thurman J. B. Austin Aaron Smith & G. W. Nichols negative none It is therefore ordered by the Court that the Trustee pay the same out of any County moneys in his hands not otherwise appropriated and that Certificate issue.

P-36 Dunlap Monday 4th Oct. 1858.

The vote of the Court being taken on an allowance of Sixty eight dollars & forty cents to S. C. Stone clerk of the County Court for services rendered the County of Sequatchee

Those who voted in the affirmative were G. W. Cain Wm B. Elliott E. S. Owings Byram Heard Edwin Newby I. N. Clark J. C. Lockhart Wm E. Kell M. B. Narrimore S. D. Thurman J. B. Austin Aron Smith & G. W. Nichols - Negative none.

It is therefore ordered by the Court that the Trustee pay the same out of any County moneys in his hands nototherwise appropriated and that Certificate issue.

The vote of the Court being taken on an allowance of fifteen dollars and sixty six cents, for making a jury room Clerks desk & C to Wm B. Elliott. Those who voted in the affirmative were G. W. Cain E. S. Owings Byram Heard Edwin Newby, I. N. Clark, J. C. Lockheart Wm E. Kell, M. B. Narrimore S. D. Thurman J. B. Austin Aaron Smith & G. W. Nichols. It is ordered by the Court that the Trustee pay the same out of any moneys in his hands not otherwise appropriated and that Certificate issue.

The vote of the Court being taken to reduce the taxes of Sequatchee County, thirteen & 1/16 per cent. on the personal & real property and fifty cents on the poll those who voted in the affirmative were G. W. Cain William B. Elliott E. S. Owings Byram Heard E. Newby Il N. Clark J. C. Lockhart Wm E. Kell, M. B. Narrimore S. D. Thurman J. B. Austin Aaron Smith and G. W. Nichols.

It is therefore ordered by the Court that the Clerk compute the taxes according to said rate.

It is ordered by the Court that the following persons be summonsed by the Shiriff of Sequatchee County, to serve as a jury of inquest for said County at December term of the Circuit Court 1858.

    Dist. 1 - A. T. Gilbreath, A. R. Thurman, Miligan Cordle
    " 2 - James B. Billingsly, C. P. Ewton
P-37 " 3 - William Stewart, M. B. Narrimore, S. D. Thurman
    " 4 - Wm Heard Wm M. Jones & Wm Johnson
    " 5 - John Farmer, Jones Mabry J. C. Lockheart
    " 6 - Thos. Hicks O. M. Thurman Wm M. Bennett
    " 7 - Jason Harvey, John Odom Simson Brock
    " 8 - Thomas King William McGlothlin
    " 9 - John C. Rickett A. H. Lockheart John Clemons.

Constables to wait on the Court
    Pleasant Johnson & M. M. Phelps

B. B. Cannon Register for Sequatchee County who was ordered by this Court to transcribe the record made by him into the Register's Book Marked Letter A presented the same, without charge which was approved by the Court.

It is ordered by the Court that Wm Williams overseer on the old Savage turnpike road be allowed to purchase the necesary tools & C, to put said road in order and to make the same a charge against the County.

Benj. Bailey who was elected Constable for the fifth Civil district of Sequatchee County presented his resignation to the Court which was accepted.

Ordered by the Court that the old Savage road leading from the Valley road on the top of Cumberland mountain be so changed as to cross Brush Creek at a better ford.

M. M. Phelps who was elected Const. on the 25th September 1858, to fill in the vacancy occasioned by the resignation of G. W. Heard, appeared into open Court and gave his bonds and took the necessary oaths for his qualification.

It appearing to the satisfaction of the Court that John Cagle is a pauper, it is therefore ordered by the Court that I. N. Clark take charge of said pauper and report to the next quarterly Court.

Ordered by the Court that J. C. Lockheart be appointed Com. on the Anderson turnpike road in the place of Wm. Barker. P-38 It appearing to the satisfaction of the Court that Elias McCarver who was put down by the revenue Com. for a poll tax, was underage. It is therefore ordered by the Court that he be released forom paying his said poll tax.

John G. Barker Henry Barker Howell Barker & Moses E. Barker Executors of the last will & testament of William Barker Dec'd appeared into open Court and presented said will which was proved by the subscribing witnesses, And the said executors entered into bond as required by law, and took the necessary oaths.

Court adjourned until tomorrow morning at 8 o'clock
  George W. Cain Chermen
  Byram Heard
  F Deakins

Court met pursuant to adjournment, There being no buisiness to transact, the Court adjourned until Court in Course.
  Byram Heard
  F. Deakins

Dunlap, Tenn, November 1st 1858.

Quorem Court met pursuant to adjournment present on the bench, Byram Heard F Deakins M. B. Narrimore, J. M. Morrison A Smith Wm E. Kell S. D. Thurman A. H. Lockheart.

G. W. Cain chairman of the Court being absent Aaron Smith was appointed in his stead, protem.

It is ordered by the Court that Isaac Johnson be appointed overseer on the public road in place of D. C. Brown , & that he have the same bounds of hands as worked under former overseer. (Iss'd)

P-39 Dunlap, Monday Nov. 1st 1858.

The executors of the will of William Barker dec'd returned into open Court an inventory if all the personal and real property of said decedent - which is ordered by the Court to be recorded.

There being no further buisiness the Court adjourned until Court in Course,
    Aaron Smith Chm
  Byram Heard F. Deakins

Dunlap, Monday Dec, 6th 1858.

Quorum Court met pursuant to adjournment. Present on the bench Esqrs G. W. Cain F. Deakins Byram Heard Aaron Smith E. S. Owings

It is ordered by the Court that the Trustee pay to Jonathan Hatfield, Coroner for Sequatchee County five dollars out of any County moneys in his hands not otherwise appropriated. for holding an inquest upon the body of Philip A. Walker, late of said County and that Certificate issue.

Court adjourned until Court in Course,
George W. Cain Cherman
Byram Heard
F. Deakins

P-40   Dunlap Tenn, Monday Jan 3rd 1859

County Court met at the Court house near Dunlap on Monday January 3rd 1859 - pursuant to adjournment.

Present on the bench G. W. Cain Byram Heard Joel B. Austin Aaron Smith S. D. Thurman M. B. Narrimore F. Deakins Wm B. Elliott Wm E. Kell J. C. Lockheart L. Hicks J. M. Morrison E. S. Owings I. N. Clark J. C. Rickett John Odom

J. M. Richards tendered his resignation to the Court which is accepted.

J. L. Hoge tendered his resignation to the County Court which was accepted.

Proclamation having been made by the Shiriff at the door of the Court house that the Court was about elect a collector of the public taxes for the year 1859, J. C. Lockheart and Howel Barker came forward and enrolled their names as candidates, and upon the first ballot J. C. Lockheart received ten votes and Howel Barker three, whereupon said Lockheart was declared duly and Constitutionally elected Collector for Sequatchee County.

The vote of the Court being taken on an allowance of seventeen dollars to George W. Cain for seventeen days at one dollar per day. and also an allowance of two dollars to Aaron Smith for acting as chairman two days at the above rate which was carried in the affirmative, It is therefore ordered by the Court that Certificate issue to them. (Iss'd)

The vote of the Court being taken on an allowance of nineteen dollars each to Byram Heard and F. Deakins for serving nineteen days as a quorem at one dollar per day, which being voted in the affirmative, It was ordered by the

P-41   Dunlap Monday Jany 3rd 1859.

Court that Certificate issue to them.

The vote of the Court being taken on an allowance of forty dollars and fifty cents to Wm Rankin for his attendance upon the County and Circuit Courts, twenty seven days at $1.50 per day, it was voted in the affirmative. It is therefore ordered by the Court that Certificate issue to him. (Iss'd)

The vote of the Court being taken on an allowance of thirteen dollars and seventy eight cents to Isaac N. Clark for necessaries furnished John Cagle a pauper within the last four months, it was carried in the affirmative. It is therefore ordered by the Court that Certificate issue to him. (Iss'd)

The vote of the Court being taken on an allowance of eight dollars and sixty seven cents, to William Williams for money expended in furnishing tools & C to work on the public roads, it was voted in the affirmative. It is therefore ordered by the Court that Certificate issue to him. (Iss'd)

The vote of the Court being taken on an allowance of twenty dollars to Burgess Taylor for services rendered in Surveying and plotting the town of Dunlap, it was carried in the affirmative. It is therefore ordered by the Court that Certificate issue to him. (Iss'd)

Ordered by the Court that James Mansfield be appointed overseer on a second class road in place of G. W. Cain Jr. and that he have the same bounds of hands as worked under former overseer. (Iss'd)

Ordered by thr Court that George W. Heard be appointed overseer on the public road in place of James Clemons and that he have the same bounds of hands as worked under former overseer. (Iss'd)

P-42   Dunlap Monday, January 3rd 1859.

It is ordered by the Court that the Trustee pay to Joseph Goulston twenty seven cents, the County tax upon one hundred dollars worth of property illegally taxed, and that Certificate issue. (Iss'd)

Ordered by the Court that Malcom Hunter be appointed overseer of the public road in place of Miligan Cordle, and that he have the same bounds of hands as worked under former overseer. (Iss'd)

The Court then proceeded to appoint F. Deakins J. B. Austin and Stephen D Thurman Commissioners to lay the taxes for the year 1859.

The vote of the Court being taken on a tax of twenty five cents on each poll for Common School purposes, it was carried in the affirmative.

The Commissioners appointed to lay the taxes for the County of Sequatchee for the year 1859 produced into Court the follwing assessment, which was confirmed by the Court.

Twenty eight and a half cents on all real and personal property, including the State tax, and one dollar and twenty five cents on _evry_ poll including the School & State tax,

              Com.   (Joel B. Austin
                        (F. Deakins
                        (S. D. Thurman

The Court then proceeded to the election of a Chairman and after several ballotings Aaron Smith was elected Chairman for the present year.

The vote of the Court was then taken upon the election of two associate Justices as a Quorem S. D. Thurmam and M. B. Narrimore was chosen.

John Clemons produced into open Court the scalp of one Wild Cat which he proved P-43 to the satisfaction of the Court was killed by him within the bounds of Sequatchee County, (Iss'd)

It is therefore ordered by the Court that Certificate issue to him.

John H, Rogers petitioned the Court for a jury of view to change the old road that runs between Joseph Davis & John H. Rogers farms, so as to run by said Davis house, which was granted. Jury of view Joseph Davis, John H. Rogers & B. B. Cannon, (Iss'd)

It appearing to the satisfaction of the Court that A. H, Lockheart has departed this life intestate, and Wm Rankin and A. J. Tate having applied for letters of administration, It is therefore ordered by the Court that letters of administration issue to them.

The vote of the Court being taken on an allowance of forty two dollars and seventy cents to J. C. Stone for services rendered the County of Sequatchee, as per orders. It was voted in the affirmative none voted in the negative, It is therefore ordered by the Court that the Clerk ussue said Certificate. (Iss'd)

The vote of the Court being taken on an allowance of one dollar to George Walker, for blank books furnished by him for the use of the County, it was granted. It is therefore ordered by the Court that Certificate issue to him. (Iss'd)

It is ordered by the Court that I. N. Clark take charge of, and furnish John Cagle, a pauper such necessaries as he ought to have, and report to the next quarterly Court.

P-44   Dunlap Monday, Jany, 3rd 1859.

The vote of the Court being taken on an allowance of twenty four dollars to S. W. Roberson for cash paid by him for advertising the sales of the town lots in Dunlap which was voted in the affimative. It is therefore ordered by the Court that Certificate issue to him. (Iss'd)

Ordered by the Court that a jury of view be appointed to change the Grayson road near Simson Brock's and report to the next term of this Court Jury of view, Simpson Brock Aarom Brimer John Picket, (Iss'd)

Ordered by the Court that the road leading from near Jesse Picketts shop to the old Laughby ford be disannulled and that the overseer and hands work on the Main Valley road under Ed Pickett. (Iss'd)

Ordered by the Court that the road leading from the Thurman turnpike road, to the Valley road near Widow Hicks be disannulled and that the hands and overseer work on the Valley road under Edward Pickett. (Iss'd)

Ordered by the Court that Edward Pickett, have all the hands on the main valley road on his section, from Thurman's Creek to the Marion County line in the Sixth Civil district on the West side of Sequatchee river. (Iss'd)

Ordered by the Court that Charles Moffat be appointed overseer on a third class road from where Wm Williams road orders stop near Mt. Pleasant meeting house, to Richard Hillis and that Bird Clark and Henry Russell work undr him. (Iss'd)

Ourdered by the Court that   be appointed to lay off to the widow of A. H.. Lockheart dec'd one years allowance & report to the next County Court.

P-45   Dunlap Monday, January 3rd 1859.

It is ordered by the Court that M. B. Narrimore take charge of, and furnish Frederick and Nancy Narramore such necessaries as they stand in need of, and report to the next quarterly Court.

The Court appointed the following persons as Revenue Com. to assess the property and polls for the County of Sequatchee for the year 1859.

Dist. 1st Aaron Smith   Dist. 5. Wm E. Kell
"   2   Joel B. Austin   "   6. J. M. Morrison
"   3   S. D. Thurman   "   7. John Odom
"   4   Wm B. Elliott   "   8. E. S. Owings
                           "   9. J. C. Rickett

Ordered by the Court that the following persons be appointed Commissioners to settle with the officers of the County - Wm. E. Kell F Deakins & S. D. Thurman.

It is ordered by the Court that the following persons be summoned be the <u>Shiriff</u> of Sequathhee County to serve as a grand jury of inquest for said County at the April term of the Circuit Court 1859.

District 1st John Welch & Joseph Turner
"   2nd E. S. Austin, Jonathan Pope John Heard
"   3   Joseph Davis Wm Brown Fo A Lanb
"   4   Wash Cain Wm B. Elliott F. Deakins
"   5   B. J. Bailey Overton Dill Wm E. Kell
"   6   Benj. Ahls Jesse Pickett J. M. Morrison
"   7   W. H. Tally David Varner Thos. Davis
"   8   John Perry Wm O. Neil Wm King
"   9   Jesse Savage & William Dugan

Constables to wait on the Court C. P. Ewton and Bird Clark.

The Court adjourned until tomorrow morning
                              Aaron Smith Chm.
                              M. B. Narrimore
                              S. D. Thurman

P-46   Dunlap Tuesday Jany 4th 1859.

Court met pursuant to adjournment Present on the bench Aaron Smith S. D. Thurman M. B. Narramore G. W. Cain.

Wm Rankin and A. J. Tate whowas appointed administrators of the estate of A. H. Lockhart dec'd appeared into open Court and gave bond as required and took the necessary oath for their qualification.

Ordered by the Court that the <u>Shiriff</u> open and hold an election in the first Civil district in Sequatchee County for one Justice of the peace & constable and also to hold an election in the fifth district for Constable. (Iss'd)

On motion of B. B. Cannon, Eli T. Sawyers was appointed deputy Register for Sequatchee County and took the necessary oaths for his qualification

Ordered by the Court that the <u>Shiriff</u> open and hold an election in the 9th Civil district of Sequatchee County for one Justice of the peace. (Iss'd)

There being no further <u>buisiness</u> the Court adjourned

until the Court in Course

        Aaron Smith Chm M. B. Narramore S. D. Thurman

P-47   Dunlap Monday Feb. 7th 1859.

Quorem Court met on this, the Seventh day of February 1859 - pursuant to adjournment,

Present on the bench Aaron Smith M. B. Narramore & S. D. Thurman.

Ordered by the Court that J. C. Wimberly be appointed overseer of the public road in place of M. M. Phelps, and that he have the same bounds of hands as worked under former overseer. (Iss'd)

Ordered by the Court that O. M. Thurman be appointed overseer of the public road from Stone's Creek to Thurman's Creek and that he have the same bounds of hands as worked under former overseer. (Iss'd)

Ordered by the Court that John Teaters be appointed overseer on the public road in place of Jas. Ewton and that he have the same bounds of hands as worked under former overseer. (Iss'd)

Ordered by the Court that Charles Lewis be appointed overseer of the public road in place of Marion Jones, and that he have the same bounds of hands as worked under former overseer. (Iss'd)

Wm. Rankin & A. J. Tate administrators of the estate of A. H. Lockheart dec'd came into Court and asked leave to make their report to the next term of this Court, which was granted. (Iss'd)

It is ordered by the Court thar Wm B. Elliott furnish Elevin Jones with such necessaries as he may think proper, Satisfactory proof having been given as to his pauperism, and that he report to the next quarterly Court the expenses.

P-48   Dunlap Monday Feb. 7th 1859.

There being no further buisiness the Court adjourned until Court in Course.
                        Aaron Smith Chm
                        S. D. Thurman
                        M. B. Narramore

Dunlap Monday 7th March 1859.

Quorem Court met pursuant to adjournment - present on the bench Aaron Smith M. B. Narramore J. C. Lockheart, J. M. Morrison & S. D. Thurman.

Aaron Brimer presented a petition for a jury of view on a third class road from near John Hoodenpyle's up the western base of Walden's ridge to the top of said mountain, then the nearest and best route to the turnpike near said Brimer which was granted. It is therefore ordered by the Court that Aaron G. Brimer John Hoodenpyle Aron Brimer Overton Dill & Joshua Easterly be appointed a jury of view to lay off and mark said road to the greatest advantage of the inhabitants and as little as may be to the predudice inclpsures - and that they report to next Court.

Wm D. Stewart tendered his resignation as Depty Shff. to the Court which was accepted.

It is ordered by the Court that the sheriff bring or cause to be brought to the next quarterly Court the following named paupers to be disposed of to the lowest bidder for the ensuing twelve months, Elevin Jones, John Cagel Frederick Narramore Rebecca Mansfield. (Iss'd)

Ordered by the Court that N. M. Lockheart be appointed overseer of a second class road P-49 in lieu of James Lockheart and that he have the same bounds of hands as worked under former overseer. (Iss'd)

It is ordered by the Court that Wm Rankin & A. J. Tate Admrs. of the estate of A. H. Lockheart dec'd have until the next Court to return an inventory of said estate, and it is also ordered that they take charge of the real estate and dispose of it to the best advantage to all concerned.

John Russell common school Com. in the eighth district tenders his resignation which is accepted. It is therefore ordered by the Court that the <u>shiriff</u> open and hold an election in said district for School com.

Ake Craig produced into open Court the scalp of one wildcat, which he proved to the satisfaction of the Court was killed by him in Sequatchee County, It is therefore ordered by the Court that Certificate issue to him.

David Hoodenpyle produced into open Court the scalp of three wild cats, which he proved to the Satisfaction of the Court was killed by him in Sequatchee County. It is therefore ordered by the Court that Certificate issue to him .

There being no further <u>buisiness</u> the Court adjourned until Court in Course.

        Aaron Smith Chm.
        S. D. Thurman
        M. B. Narramore

P-50 Dunlap Monday 4th April 1859.

The wroshipful County Court for the County of Sequatchee

36.

met at the Court house in the town of Dunlap Monday the 4th Apl. 1859 - pursuant to adjournment.

Present on the bench Esqrs. A. Smith S. D. Thurman M. B. Narramore Wm E. Kell Wm. B. Elliott G. W. Cain E. S. Owings J. B. Austin J. M. Morrison & Byram Heard Jno. Odom A. J. Tate I. N. Clark F. Deakins J. C. Lockheart.

Ordered by the Court that the road leading from the Valley road on the East side of the river to the Gap, be reduced to a fourth class road, and also that S. W. Roberson be authorized to open and keep up a third class road from the Valley road on the west side of the river from near George Walker's to Roberson's mill. and that he be authorized to put gates on said road, upon which he is to be the overseer and have his own hands to work on said road, and that he have one month to put said road in order. (Iss'd)

Ordered by the Court that Wm Williams work his road only to the Cliff of the mountain.

The vote of the Court being taken on an allowance of four dollars and seventy five cents to Wm B. Elliott for necessaries furnished Elevin Jones, as a pauper, as per order of Court, It was voted in the affirmative - It is therefore ordered by the Court that Certificate issue to him. (Iss'd)

The vote of the Court being taken on an allowance of fifteen dollars and ninety four cents to M. B. Narramore for necessaries furnished his father and mother Fredrick and Nancy Narramore as paupers was voted in the affirmative. (Iss'd)

It is ordered by the Court that Certificate issue to him. The vote of the Court being taken on an allowance of six dollars to each revenue Com. for the year 1859 for taking down the taxable property in their respective districts to wit A. Smith W. B. Elliott S. D. Thurman J. B. Austin Wm. E. Kell J. M. Morrison John Odom E. S. Owings & J. C. Ricket. It is therefore ordered by the Court that Certificate issue to them.

P-51   Dunlap, Monday 4th April 1859.

A. J. Tate, who was elected Justice of the peace for the Ninth Civil district of Sequatchee County in the place of A. H. Lockheart dec'd, appeared into open Court and gave bond & took the oaths necessary to his qualification.

The vote of the Court being taken on an allowance of twenty dollars sixteen cents to I. N. Clark for furnishing John Cagle a pauper with the necessaries of life. It was voted in the affirmative. (Iss'd)

The vote of the Court being taken on an allowance of one dollar per day to the Chairman of the County Court for the year 1858, to G. W. Cain seventeen days & Aaron Smith, two days, - It was voted in the affirmative. It is therefore ordered by the Court that Certificate issue to them. (Iss'd)

The vote of the Court being taken on an allowance of five dollars to Aaron Smith for books furhished by him for County purposes. It was voted in the affirmative, It is therefore ordered by the Court that Certificaate issue to him. (Iss'd)

Ordered by the Court that the road leading across the mountain be changed from a second to a third class road from A. J. Tate's to Warren County line.

Ordered by the Court that Reuben Hixson be appointed overseer of third class road from the end of Gott's & Anderson's lane to Anderson's mill - in the place of James I. Rogers, & that he have the same bounds ofhands as worked under former overseer, except the hands attached to the mountain road.

P-52   Dunlap, Monday, 4th April 1859.

Rebecca Mansfield, a pauper, who was ordered to be let out to the lowest bidder, was cried off by the Sheriff, and John C. Lockheart being the lowest bidder, she was let off to him for seventy five dollars for twelve months. (Iss'd)

Wm Rankin & A. J. Tate administrators of the estate of A. H. Lockheart dec'd returned into open Court an inventory of the estate of said Lockheart, and a list of sale of said Lockheart, and a list of sale of said estate duly authenticated, which was ordered to be recorded.

The vote of the Court being taken on an allowance of twenty five cents,- to J. B. Austin Wm B. Elliott Wm. D. Kell J. M. Morrison John Odom, E. S. Owings & John C. Rickett for books furnished as revenue commissioners. It was carried in the affirmative. (Iss'd)

M. M. Phelps tendered his resignation as Const. of the fourth Civil district of Sequatchee County which is accepted. M. M. Phelps & Isaac Hicks who was appointed Deputy Shiriffs appeared into open Court and took the necessary oaths for their qualification.

Joseph White produced into open Court the scalp of one wild cat, which he prooved to the satisfaction of the Court was killed by him in Sequatchee County. It is therefore ordered by the Court that certificate issue to him. (Iss'd)

David Hoodenpyle who had proved the scalps of three wild cats in the County Court, was allowed three dollars and seventy five cents to be paid out of the County treasury. It is ordered that Certificate issue to him. (Iss'd)

P-53   Dunlap, Monday, 4th April 1859

Commissioners appointed to examine and report to the next term quarterly Court, the condition of the paupers of Sequatchee County, and also to furnish them with Such necessaries as they actually stand in need of, and present their acct. to said Court.

    Coms for Fredrick & Nancy Narrimore,
        Dr. John W. Simpson & Wm Stewart,
    Coms for John Cagle
        John C. Rickett   I. M. Clark
    Coms for Elevin Jones
        Wm B. Elliott & Geo. Walker,
    Coms for Robert Taylor
        John Bennett, & Ephraim Thurman

Burgess Taylor who was Surveyor for Sequatchee County having left the Country the Court ordered an election for Surveyor, John H. Rogers and Alfred Davis being candidates, Rogers received the entire vote and was thereupon declared duly elected Surveyor for said County for the term of four years.

The vote of the Court being taken on an allowance of two dollars and fifty cents to the Justices attending the County Court at quarterly terms from July till April 1859 - towit, at Jany term.
    G. W. Cain Byram Heard Joel B. Austin Aaron Smith S. D. Thurman M. B. Narramore F Deakins Wm B. Elliott Wm E. Kell J. C. Lockheart T. Hocks J. M. Morrison E. S. Owings I. N, Clark J. C. Rickett & John Odom.

April term
    Aaron Smith M. B. Narramore, S. D. Thurman Wm E. Kell Wm B. Elliott G. W. Cain E. S. Owings J. B. Austin J. Morrison Byram Heard John Odom A. J. Tate I.N. Clark F Deakins J. C. Lockheart.

Ordered by the Court that the Shff. open and hold an election in the 4Civil district of Sequatchee County for Constable in lieu of M. M. Phelps resigned.

P-54 J. C. Lockheart who was elected Collector of the public revenue for Sequatchee County for the year 1859 by the County Court at its Jany term 1859 appeared into Court and gave bonds and took the necessary oath for his qualification.

Collectors Bond
State
    Know all men by these presents that we J. C. Lockheart Jesse Pickett Joshua Easterly Isaac Hicks & John Pickett are held and firmly bound unto the State of Tennessee in the sum of fiteen hundred dollars, Sealed with our Seals and dated the 4th day of April 1859-

The condition of the above obligation is such that whereas the above bound J. C. Lockheart was, at the January term of the County Court 1859 duly elected Collector of the public revenue for the year 1859.

If therefore the Said John C. Lockheart shall faithfully collect & pay over to the Treasurer of the State, all State taxes by him collected or which ought to be collected against the last day of Dec$\underline{r}$ 1859,

Then this obligation to be void, otherwise to remain in full force & effect - This day & date above written,

    Approved by me   John C. Lockheart   SEAL
    S. C. Stone, Clerk   his
                                Jesse x Pickett   SEAL
                                    mark
                                Joshua Easterly   SEAL
                                Isaac Hicks   SEAL
                                John Pickett   SEAL

                     Collectors Bond

County

Know all men by these presents that we John C. Lockheart Jesse Pickett Joshua Easterly Isaac Hicks John Pickett are held and firmly bound unto the State of Tennessee in the sum of fifteen hundred dollars fro which sum we bind ourselves jointly & severally by these presents, Sealed with our Seals & dated the 4th day of April 1859-

The condition of the above obligation is such that whereas the above bound J. C. Lockheart was elected Collector of public revenue for Sequatchee County, for the year 1859.

P-55   Dunlap Monday 4th April 1859.

Now if the said John C. Lockheart shall faithfully collect & pay over to the Trustee of Said County, all County tax by him collected, or which ought to be collected against the last day of Dec$\underline{r}$ 1859-

Then this obligation to be void otherwise to remain in full force and effect, This day & date above written,

    Approved by me   John C. Lockheart   SEAL
    S. C. Stone, Clerk   his
                                  Jesse x Pickett   SEAL
                                    mark
                                Joshua Easterly   SEAL
                                Isaac Hicks   SEAL
                                John Pickett   SEAL

                     Collectors Bond

School

Know all men by these presents that we John C, Lockheart Jesse Pickett Joshua Easterly Isaac Hicks and John Pickett are held and firmly bound unto the State of Tennessee in the sum of two thousand dollars for the payment of which sum we bind ourselves jointly & severally by these presents.

Sealed with our Seals & dated this 4th April 1859.

The condition of the above obligation is such that whereas the above bound J. C. Lockheart, was by the County Court elected Collector of the public revenue for Sequatchee County for the year 1859.

If therefore the said J. C. Lockheart shall faithfully collect and pay over to the County Trustee all school moneys by him collected, whether levied on behalf of the State, or of the County, according to law.

Then this obligation to be void otherwise to run on in full force and & effect, This day & date above written.

  Approved by me John C. Lockheart SEAL
  S. C. Stone,   his
   Clerk   Jesse x Bickett SEAL
           mark
         Joshua Easterly SEAL
         Isaac Hicks SEAL
         John Pickett SEAL

P-56 Dunlap Tenn, Monday, 4th April 1859.

Ordered by the Court that Jonathan Turner be appointed overseer of the Public road from B. L. Bennett's to the Southern County line and that he have the same bounds of hands as worked under former overseer. (Iss'd)

  Report of Jury of view.

We the undersigned Jury of view appointed by the Court to view the road between John H. Rogers and Joseph Davis, do report that we think it expedient to change the road to run from the ford near the mouth of Brush Creek, up Sequatchee river to Davis apple orchard, then through the lane Strait by said Davis house to intersect the other road at the Blacksmith shop This 20th Jany 1859.

    John H. Rogers
    B. B. Cannon
    Joseph Davis

  Report of Jury of View.

We the undersigned have viewed and marked out a road agreeable to the within order This ____ day of March 1859- John W. Hoodenpyle A. G. Brimer Aron Brimer Overton Dill.

  Report of Jury of view

We the undersigned have viewed and changed the road according to the within order, 26th March 1859
   Cimpson Brock Aron Brimer John Picket

Ordered by the Court that John W. Hoodenpyle be appointed overseer on a third class road from near his house to the turnpike road near Aron Brimer's and that he have Overton Dill John Winder Amos Briner Wilson L. Brimer Isaac Fredrick's Franklin Fredrick John Reel Rm Brown Aaron Brimer to work on said road

P-57 Dunlap Tuesday, 5th April 1859
State of Tennessee) County Court, April term
Sequatchee County) 1859

We the Commissioners appointed by the County Court at the January term did proceed to lay a tax on lands and towns lots and slaves and polls, We do further proceed to lay a tax upon all persons for retailing patent medicines $5.00. Evry pedler furnishing patent medicines $10.00. Stallions & jacks the same as State tax, Merchants ¼ per cent or twenty five cents on the hundred dollars worth of merchandise at the invoice cost where purchased. Grocery keepers, pedlers and all persons using a privalege the Same, as State tax, All Suits in Court the same as State tax, Joel Be. Austin
F. Deakins
S. D. Thurman

William Johnson was appointed by the Court Standard Keeper & Sealer of Weights & measures for the County of Sequatchee,

The Court appointed five Trustees for the Rankin Academy for the ensuing two years, to wit, Joshua Easterly George W. Cain Sam'l W. Roberson William D. Stewart & Thompson Hicks. (Iss'd)

Court adjourned until tomorrow morning at 9 o'clock
Aaron Smith Chm
S. D. Thurman
M. B. Narramore

Ordered by the Court that the Sheriff open and hold an election in the third civil district of Sequatchee County for Constable.

P-58 Dunlap Tuesday - 5th Apl. /59

William Johnson who was appointed Standard Keeper & Sealer of Weights & measures appeared into open Court and took the oath required by law,-

Ordered by the Court that Ephraim Thurman be required to furnish Elizabeth Carmack a pauper with such necessaries as she requires, and report to the next quarterly Court,

There being no further buisiness the Court adjourned until Court in Course,
Aaron Smith Chm
S. D. Thurman
M. B. Marramore

Dunlap, Monday 2nd May 1859.

Quorem Court met pursuant to adjournment. Present on the bench Esqrs. Smith Thurman & Narramore.

It is ordered by the Court that Burrel Barker be appointed overseer on the public road in place John Heard & that he have the same bounds of hands as worked under former overseer. (Iss'd)

Oliver M. Hatfield who was elected Constable for the fourth Civil district of Sequatchee Tennessee on the 30th April 1859 - appeared into open Court and gave bonds and took the oath of office and entered upon the discharge of his duties.

It is ordered by the Court that the following persons be summons by the Sheriff of Sequatchee County, to serve as a grand jury of Inquest for said County, at the August term of the Circuit Court 1859.

P-59   Dunlap Monday May 2nd 1859.
Venire

District 1st - Walter B. Kennedy Jefferson Walker Hezikiah Harvey
" 2nd - Josiph Minton Philip Hoots, & Byram Heard.
" 3rd - F. J. Johnson Sames Jones & Houston Barker
" 4 - J. R. Brown Wm Phelps James W. Hatfield.
" 5 - John Hoodenpyle Joseph Easterly Peter Brown.
" 6 - M. P. D. Stone John Frizzelle & John F. Heron.
" 7 - Washington Porter & John Kell Sr. David Brown.
" 8 - E. S. Owings & I. N. Clark
" 9 & A. J. Tate & James Lockheart

The Court also orders that Certificate issue Constables to wait on Court C. M. Hatfield John Lewis

The Court then adjourned until Court in Course
Aaron Smith Chm.
S. D. Thurman
M. B. Narramore

Dunlap June 6th 1859.

Quorem Court met pursuant to adjournment. Present on the bench Esqrs. Aaron Smith S. D. Thurman & M. B. Narramore.

Leonard Lewis produced into open Court the scalp of one wolf which he proved to the Satisfaction of the Court was killed by him in Sequatchee County, Tennessee. It is therefore ordered by the Court that the Treasurer of the State of Tennessee pay to Said Lewis Six dollars according to act of assembly. (Iss'd)

The Court appointed the following persons Trustees of the Rankin Academy of Sequatchee County, for the Ensuing two years, J. W. Simpson S. D. Thurman F. Deakins J. R. Brown and

William Rankin, who appeared into Court and was qualified to faithfully discharge the duties incumbent on them according to law. (Academy Iss(d)

P-60   Dunlap, Monday June 6th 1859.

Ordered by the Court that John Pickett be appointed overseer of a third class road in Sequatchee County, leading from Grayson's Gap to the Anderson turnpike road and that he have the following hand to work on said road, to wit, H. Doolen, M. Vandergriff Jacob Vandergriff Joseph Winchester Aaron Newbern Henry Peacock & Simpson Brock. (Iss'd)

The Clerk of the Court presented to the Court the Certified bill of cost which accrued in the Circuit Court in the case of the State vs. C. P. Ewton in which case a verdict of not guilty was found by the jury - it was ordered by the Circuit Court that the County pay the cost of said suit, which proceedings was ordered by the Court to be spread of record it as follows,

State of Tennessee)   The defendant having been
    vs   )   acquitted and discharged at
C. P. Ewton   )   the last term of the Circuit
Court the following bill of cost on the part of the State which accrued in the cause have been examined & allowed and are ordered by the Court to be entered on the record and it is further ordered by the Court that they be paid out of the County Treasury, to wit,

```
        State tax                        2.00
Clerk J. L. Stone entering
        indictment              .25
docketing cause, 10¢ issuing
        capias                  .75
Subpiena for 5 witnesses, 50,
empannelling jury 10, ent-
ering Judg.75 entering bill
of cost on execution docket   .50    2.95
Sheriff Rankin arrest 1.00
taking bond .25 Summoning
five witnesses      1.25              2.50
Witnesses, John Teaters - one day    .75
        Bytam Heard  -   "    "      .75
        Roderick Rogers  "    "      .75
        Philip Hoots     "    "      .75
        Thos. Minton     "    "      .75
Attorney Genl fee                    2.50
                                    ─────
                                    13.70
```

P-61   Dunlap, Monday June 6th 1859
I, certify that the above bill of cost is legally and correctly taxed as appears upon the record in my office
            J. L. Stone, Clerk
We have examined the foregoing bill of cost and believe the same to be correctly taxed.

Wm C. Payne
Attorney Genl.
E. L. Gardenhire, Judge

John Henson Produced into Court a Certified copy of his appointment as guardian of the minor heirs of James Heard dec'd and also his guardian bond which was taken in Hamilton County, for the purpose of removing said guardianship to this Court, which is ordered by the Court to be recorded. It is as follows - (Iss'd)

State of Tennessee to wit at a County Court begun and held for the County of Hamilton at the Court house in the town of Harrison on the first Monday and fifth day of October in the year of Our Lord one thousand eight hundred and fifty seven on Wednesday of said Court John F. White Judge & C presiding were the following proceedings.
John Henson Guardian.

The Court appointed John Henson guardian to Levander Heard Susan Heard and Martha Heard, who came ihto Court and entered into bond of four thousand dollars - was duly qualified and gave as his security Wm R. Henson John Heard and John Anderson which bond was examined and approved by the Court, and ordered of record & filed, which bonds are in the words & figures following, to wit,

State of Tennessee) We John Henson William R. Henson
Hamilton County) & John Heard & John Anderson are held and firmly bound unto John F. White Judge of the County Court for the County aforesaid and his successors in office, in the sum of four thousand dollars in trust for the use & benefit of the children heretofore named & committed to the tuition of the said John Henson for which payment well and truly to be made, we bind ourselves our heirs executors administrators   P-62   jointly and Severally by these presents Sealed with our Seals and dated the 5th day of Oct. 1857.

The condition of the above obligation is such that whereas the above bounden John Henson is constituted and appointed guardian to Levander Heard Susan Heard & Martha Heard minor orphands, Now if the Said John Henson Shall faithfully execute his guardianship by securing and improving all the estate of his said wards, that Shall come into his possession for the benefit of the Said minors, until they shall have arrived at full age and shall also at the next County Court, held for the County aforesaid, exhibit and account upon oath, of all the estate of said Orphans, which he shall have received into his hands or possession and shall thereafter annually make settlement with the Clerk of the County Court of the County aforesaid, as to the profits and disbursements of the estate of said orphans upon oath as required by law, then this obligation to be void or else to remain in full force & virtue, Given under our hands & seals this date above

      John Henson SEAL
  Wm R. Henson SEAL John Heard SEAL
     John Anderson SEAL

  State of Tennessee) I Geo W. Arnett Clerk of the
  Hamilton County) County Court of said County,
do certify that the foregoing is a full and complete copy of
the records of the appointment of John Henson guardian to
the minor orphans of _____Heard dec'd, and also a copy of
the bond given by Said Henson as the same remain on file
and of record in Said Court.
     In testimony whereof I have hereunto set my
SEAL OF OFFICE hand and seal of office at office in Harri-
     son the 9th day of May 1859
        Geo W. Arnett, Clk.

  Whereupon Said Henson was appointed Guardian for said
minors by this Court and entered into another bond with
Jonathan Pope J. W. Simpson & Wm Rankin as his Securities
in the sum of four thousand dollars. which was approved by
the Court and ordered to be recorded and was qualified according to law.

P-63   Dunlap Monday June 6th 1859.

  The petition of Wm Rankin, for a jury of view to mark out
and locate a road of the second class to some point on Sequatchee river between the mouths of Brush Coops Creek suitable to
build a bridge across said river, from Dunlap to the valley
road on the East side of Sequatchee river was granted, and
John H. Rogers Wm. D. Stewart J. R. Brown Wm. B. Elliott &
F. Deakins was appointed as said Jury. (Iss'd)

  It appearing to the satisfaction of the Court that Mary
Deakins has departed this life intestate and that Franklin
Deakins Is entitled to the administration, It is therefore
ordered by the Court that he be appointed administrator of
said estate, Whereupon he came into Court and entered into
bond with approved security in the sum of one hundred and
fifty dollars for the faithful performance of said duties
and was qualified according to law.

  Eli Hatfield produced into open Court the scalp of one
Wild cat which he proved to the satisfaction of the Court
was kill by him in Sequatchee County. It is therefore ordered by the Court that Certificate issue to him. (Iss'd)

  John Lewis produced into Court the scalp of one wild cat
which he proved to the Satisfaction of the Court was killed
by him in Sequatchee County. It is therefore ordered by the
Court that Certificate issue to him. (Iss'd)

   Ordered by the Court that they adjourn until Court in
Course   _____ Aaron Smith Chm

S. D. Thurman
M. B. Narramore

P-64   Dunlap, July 4th 1859.

The quarterly County Court for the County of Sequatchee and State of Tennessee met at the Court house in the town of Dunlap on this the 4th of July 1859. Present on the bench Esqrs. Aaron Smith, S. D. Thurman M. B. Narramore Wm E. Kell I. N. Clark, J. M. Morrison F. Deakins G. W. Cain E. S. Owings, J. B. Austin, William B. Elliott J. C. Rickett, John Odom T. Hicks Byram Heard J. C. Lockheart.

B. W. Roberson petitioned the Court for third class road from the Valley road on the East side of Sequatchee river to run through the Wheeler & Welch lane to his mill, and also for the privelidge of erecting a gate on said road on his own land across said road - which was granted, - It is therefore ordered by the Court that said road be opened, and that Sam'l W. Roberson be appointed overseer on said and have his own hands to work on it.

Wm Rankin Sheriff returned into Court a report of a jury of view to locate a road, to some suitable place on Sequatchee river to build a bridge across said river, which report is in the following words

We as Jurors of view being legally summoned and sworn have proceeded to Survey and mark out a road as directed within, leaving the old where the path turns out and leading by J. R. Brown's house follwoing Said path in the Main and topping Sequatchee river opposite the lower end of John Cannon's field, and intersecting the old road again near the upper corner of Jo. Roger's field, this 18th June 1859. Wm B. Elliott, F. Deakins Wm. D. Stewart J. H. Rogers J. R. Brown which report being unaccepted to is in all things confirmed.

Wm Rankin Shff returned into Court a road order to John Picket, with the following endorsement, Executed by delivering a true copy June 29th 1859 Wm Rankin Shff.

John Fredricks presented to the Court a petition to disannulled a third class road leading from near John Hoodenply's to intersect the old turnpike P-65 road near Aaron Brimer's the vote of the Court being taken upon Said petition it was decided to let the road Stand.

The vote of the Court being taken on an allowance to Eph Thurman of eighteen dollars and forty two cents for furnishing Mrs. Carmack, a pauper, necessaries - it was voted in the affirmative. (Iss'd)

The vote of the Court being taken on an allowance of Sixten dollars and forty cents, to I. N. Clark for furnishing necessaries to John Cagle a pauper as per order of Court. It was voted in the affirmative. (Iss'd)

The vote of the Court being taken on an allowance of twenty four dollars and forty five cents to Wm. B. Elliott for furnishing Eleven Jones - a pauper, the necessaries of life, it was voted in the affirmative. (Iss'd)

The vote of the Court being taken on an allowance of fifteen dollars and fifty four cents to Wm Stewart for furnishing Fredrick Narramore & Nancy Narramore the necessaries of life, as per order of the Court. It was voted in the affirmative. (Iss'd)

The vote of the Court being taken on an allowance of two dollars and fifty cents, to the Justices of the peace for attending the quarterly term of this Court. It was voted in the affirmative. M. B. Narramore Wm E. Kell, I. N. Clark. J. M. Morrison F. Deakins G. W. Cain E. S. Owings J. B. Austin Wm B. Elliott, J. C. Ricket John Odom T. Hicks, Byram Heard J. C. Lockheart. (Iss'd)

It was ordered by the Court that the paupers of the County of Sequatchee be cryed off by the Sheriff at the Court house door in the town of Dunlap instanter to the lowest bidder for the term of six months, which was done accordingly - Henritta Griffith took Mrs. Carmack for the sum of thirty four dollars and entered into bond with Eph Thurman as security in the sum of sixty eight dollars for the performance of her contract.

P-66   Dunlap Monday, July 4th 1859.

I. N. Clark being the lowest bidder for John Cagle he was knocked off to him for the sum of Seventy five dollars.

Eleven Jones was then let off to M. M. Phelps he being the lowest bidder, for the sum of Seventy five dollars.

The vote of the Court being taken on an allowance of fifty one dollars and eighty cents to S. C. Stone for services rendered as clerk of the County Court. It was voted in the affirmative. (Iss'd)

John Clemons produced into Court the scalp of one wild cat which he proved to the Satisfaction of the Court waskilled by him in Sequatchee County. It is therefore ordered by the Court that Certificate issue to him. (Iss'd)

On motion of M. B. Narramore J. M. Stewart was nominated for County Commissioner to examine and license teachers of the Common schools - whereupon the Court proceeded to ballot which resulted as follows J. M. Stewart received nine votes and W. D. Stewart received five voted J. M. Stewart was declared elected for the present year.

It is ordered by the Court that Wm Stewart take charge of and furnish Fredrick Narramore & Nancy Narramore such necessaries as they may require and report to the next quarterly Court.

Ordered by the Court that Wm B. Elliott take charge of and furnish Eleven Jones a pauper such necessaries as he may be in need of - and report the expenses to the next quarterly Court.

Ordered by the Court that Sam'l W. Roberson S. C. Stone Wm Phelps Edwin Newby Wm Rankin County Com. to superintend the erection of the public P-67 buildings & C present a plan of a jail to the next quarterly Court for its consideration.

The Court appointed the following persons as Judges to hold an election for Governor. Members of Congress and Members to the State legislature.

```
Dist. 1 - Miligan Cordle
  "   2 - Jonathan Pope    Thos. Minton
  "   3 - Howel Barker John Cannon Wm Brown
  "   4 - Wm Johnson Madison Deakins Jas. W. Hatfield
  "   5 - Joshua Easterly Jones Mabry T. J. Hoodenpyle
  "   6 - Thos. Hicks J. M. Morrison Jas. Farmer
  "   7 - David Varner Allen Gray David Brown
  "   8 - Littleton Cagle Chas. Moffitt I. N. Clark
  "   9 - Jesse Savage Jas. Lockheart Jackson Tate
```

Ordered by the Court that the road leading from J. M. Morrison Shop, Laugby ford be revived, and that Albert Sanders be appointed overseer of Said road, and that he have all the hands on Benj, Alls farm & Jesse Picketts river farm on the west side to work on Said road.

J. B. Austin offered his resignation to the Court as Justice of the Peace which was accepted.

It is ordered by the Court that the first and second district of Sequatchee County be consolidated and that it be denominated the first district and the voting place to be at A. R. Thurmans.

It is ordered by the Court that the Ninth Civil district of Sequatchee County, be changed and known hereafter as the Second district,

Ordered by the Court that Wm Rankin have leave to erect two gates across his lane leading to the mountain.

There being no further buisiness the Court adjourned

until, Court in Course.

                      Aaron Smith Chm.
                      S. P. Thurman
                      M. B. Narramore

P-68   Dunlap, Monday, Aug. 1st 1859.

    Quorum Court met pursuant to adjournment, present on the bench Esqrs. Aaron Smith S. D. Thurman M. B. Narramore.

    M. M. Phelps & Lewis Carlton com. appointed to lay of to the widow of A. H. Lockheart decd. one years allowance, returns their order with the following endorsement upon it.

    We the com. appointed by the County Court to lay off a years allowance to the widow of A. H. Lockheart decd. proceeded to the duty assigned us Jany. 1859. and after examining the property which was exempt and we allow her fifty dollars out of the estate of said Lockheart decd. M. M. Phelps Lewis Carlton.

    Wm Rankin Sheriff returned into Court one road order to Albert Sanders, with the following endorsement, "Executed by delivering a true copy of the within
        July 16th 1859 - Wm Rankin Shff.

    Wm Rankin, Shff. returned into Court a venire facias with the following endorsement, "Executed on all the within named Jurors, and Constables in due time by summoning them in person. and leaving written summons at their place of residence, returned this Aug. 1st 1859 - Wm Rankin Shff.

    Nancy Davis alias Nancy Heard returned into Court an account of the money collected by her as administratrix of the extate of James Heard decd. sworn to and Subscribed August 1st 1859, which statement is in the words and figures following to wit,

Received	of Alfred King	.25
"	" A. J. Nichols	1.00
"	" Houston Wheeler	.15
"	" Joel Hoge	.80
"	" J. Jones	.35
"	" Wm R. Henson	3.00
"	" G. W. Cain	.50
"	" Wm Johnson by John McWilliams	10.00
"	" John M. Hixson	4.15
"	" N. M. Pope	1.50
"	" Thos. Sunns per McWilliams	16.66
"	" Andrew Bowman	1.40
"	" John Horn per McWilliams	3.70
"	" John Henson	4.00
"	" James Jones	3.00
"	" Harvey Sparger	14.50
"	" J. H. Hatfield	4.15
"	" Jo. A. Lamb	43.00

State of Tennessee) I Nancy Davis administratrix
Sequatchee County) of the estate of James Heard
decd. certify that the following report is true to the best
of my knowledge and belief, This 1st Aug. 1859.

              her
Sworn to in open Court   Nancy x Davis
August 1st 1859   mark
 S. C. Stone Clk.

A Settlement of Nancy Heard administratrix of the estate of James Heard decd. made with the clerk of the County Court of Marion having been presented to the Court for its action. It is ordered to be recorded.

Lewis Carlton produced into open Court the scalp of two wild cats which he proved to the Satisfaction of the Court was killed by him in Sequatchee County, It is therefore ordered that Certificate issue to him.

J. C. Rickett produced into open Court the scalp of two wild cats which he proved to the satisfaction of the Court was killed by him in Sequatchee County. It is therefore ordered that Certificate issue to him.

P-70   Dunlap Monday August 1st 1859.

Charles Cagle produced into open Court the scalp of one wild cat which he proved to the satisfaction of the Court was killed by him in Sequatchee County. It is therefore ordered by the Court that Certificate issue to him. (Iss'd)

William Johnson petitioned the Court to legitimate a child, which petition is in the following words,

To the worshipful County Court now in Session, your petitioner would request unto your worshipful body, that some time prior to his marriage with his wife Harriett Heard they had a child born to them, to wit, Rebecca Jane, and some time after said illegitimate child was born your petitioner intermarried with said Harriett Heard.

The premises considered your petitioner prays that your worshipful body will grant an order or decree ligitimating said child, Rebecca Janes, restoring her to all the rights and privaliges of a child born in lawful wedlock Ausust 1st
1859   Wm Johnson

Which petition being fully understood by the Court it is ordered that Said petition be granted. and that Said illegitimate child Rebecca Jane be restored to all rights and privaliges of a legal heir at law.

William Carlton produced into open Court the scalp of one wild cat which he proved to the Satisfaction of the Court was killed by him in Sequatchee County. It is therefore ordered by the Court that Certificate issue to him. (Iss'd)

Ordered by the Court that they adjourn until Court in Course,
          Aaron Smith Chm.
          S. D. Thurman
          M. B. Narramore

P-71   Dunlap Sept. 5th 1859.

Quorum Court met pursuant to adjournment. Present on the bench the worshipful Aaron Smith chairman S. D. Thurman and M. B. Narramore.

It is ordered by the Court that the following persons be Summonsed by the Sheriff of Sequatchee County, to serve as Jurors at the December term of the Circuit Court 1859 for Sequatchee County.

    Dist. 1 - Aaron Smith, S. W. Roberson Garrett Smith James M. Ewton
    " 2 - James Clemons, V. M. Lockheart
    " 3 - John H. Rogers, S. D. Thurman, M. B. Narramore, Wm. D. Stewart
    " 4 - George Walker, sen. Robert Mansfield, George W. Cain, Pleasant Johnson.
    " 5 - James I. Rogers, B. L. Bennett J. G. Barker & Robt. Reynolds.
    " 6 - James S. Farmer, John Griffith, Thos. Pankey
    " 7 - Washington Coleman, Aaron Brimer
    " 8 - Thomas Barnes & Wm Williams

Harvey Hendrix and James Tate are appointed to wait on the Court.

Wm Williams returns his road order with proof of the good order of said road and the Court appointed Andrew King to act as overseer in his stead, to have the same bounds as worked under former overseer. (Not iss'd)

Ordered by the Court that A. J. Barnes be appointed overseer of a public road in place of Wm O'Neal and have the same bounds of hands as worked under former overseer, said road being a third class road. (Iss'd)

Wm Rankin Sheriff of Sequatchee County tenders his resignation which is to take effect from and after the first Monday in Oct. 1859.

P-72   Dunlap Monday Sept. 5th 1859.

William Smith returned his road order which is rec'd and Charles Barnes is appointed overseer of said road it being a third class road, and to have the same bounds of hands to work on said road as worked under former overseer. (Iss')

Washington Coleman produced into Court the scalp of one Wild cat which he proved to the Satisfaction of the Court was killed by him in Sequatchee County. It is therefore ordered by the Couert that Certificate issue to him. (Iss'd)

David Brown produced into open Court the scalp of one Wild cat which he proved to the Satisfaction of the Court was killed by him in Sequatchee County. It is therefore ordered by the Court that Certificate issue to him. (Iss'd)

Howel Barker Collector of the taxes for Sequatchee County for the year 1858, returned to the Court the following list of delinquent tax payers.

John Mazy,	1 poll	$1.25	Reuben Brown	1 poll	1.25
J. W. Hoge	1 "	1.25	Sam'l Cheek	1 "	1.25
Sampson Ewton	"	1.25	James Terry	1 "	1.25
Eleven Roarkl	"	1.25	John Pickett	1 "	1.25
Jerry Roark	1 "	1.25	Aarom Brimer	1 "	1.25
Lea Brown,	Jewelry	1.33	Thomas Priddy	1 "	1.25
Elias McCarver	"	1.25	Jacob Coulston	1 "	1.25
Fountain Davis	"	1.25	Rheuben Brown	1 "	1.25
Stephen Deakins	"	1.25	E. G. Childers	1 "	1125
Wm. Kent	1 "	1.25	Wm Odom	1 "	1.25
Wm. Odom	1 "	1.25			31.33
Edward Card	1 "	1.25			
Thomas A. Jones	"	1.25			
James McClurel	"	1.25			
N. Turner	1. "	1.25			

State of Tennessee)
Sequatchee County)
I Howel Barker Collector of the public taxes for the County aforesaid for the year 1858, do certify P-73 that the above is a true statement of the delinquent tax payers, which I was unable to collect.

  Sworn to before me)   Howel Barker
  S. C. Stone Clerk)

It is therefore ordered by the Court that Said Howel Barker colledtor as aforesaid be released from paying Said amt. of thirty one dollars and thirty three cents.

It is ordered by the Court that all the roads in Sequatchee County, upon which the Court have placed overseers and hands to work, be established and confirmed by this order.

It appearing to the Satisfaction of the Court that Patience Rogers has departed this life intestate, and that Josiah Rogers is entitled to the administration, It is therefore ordered by the Court that he be appointed administrator of the estate of said intestate.

Josiah Rogers who was appointed administrator of the estate of Patience Rogers deceased appeared into open Court and gave bond with approved security, in the sum of one hundred dollars, and was duly qualified according to law.

Josiah Rogers admr. of the estate of Patience Rogers decd.

entered into Court an inventory of said estate duly certified which being fully understood by the Court is ordered to be recorded.

   Ordered that Court adjourn until Court in Course,
    Aeron Smith chm. S. D. Thurman, M. B. Narramore.

P-74   Dunlap Monday Oct. 3rd 1859.

The County Court for the County of Sequatchee met pursuant to adjournment. Present on the bench Esqrs. Aaron Smith M. B. Narramore Wm B. Elliott G. W. Cain E. S. Owings Edwin Newby F. Deakins A. J. Tate J. C. Rickett I. N. Clark Wm E. Kell J.M. Morrison Thompson Hicks John Odom and J. C. Lockheart.

S. D. Thurman one of the quorum not being present the Court appointed Wm B. Elliott to act in his stead.

The vote of the Court being taken on an allowance of forty dollars to William Rankin for Services rendered as Sheriff of Sequatchee County, in holding Courts and Summoning Jurors, It was voted in the affirmative. It is therefore ordered by the Court that Certificate issue to him. (Iss'd)

The vote of the Court being taken on an allowance of nineteen dollars and sixty six cents to William B. Elliott for furnishing Eleven Jones & wife necessaries as per order of Court- It was voted in the affirmative. It is therefore ordered by the Court that Certificate issue to him. (Iss'd)

The vote of the Court being taken on an allowance of Seventeen dollars and eighty eight cents to William Stewart for furnishing Fred Narramore necessaries of life as per order of Court. It was voted in the affirmative. It is therefore ordered by the Court that Certificate issue to him. (Iss'd)

It is ordered by the Court that Wm Stewart take charge of and furnish F. Narramore such necessaries of life as he may actually stand in need of, and report the charges to the next quarterly Court.

P-75   Dunlap Monday 3rd Octr 1859.

Ordered by the Court that Gilbert Hatfield take charge of and furnish Eleven Jones & wife such necessaries as they actually stand in need of until the first Monday in January next, for the sum of twenty dollars.

Ordered by the Court that Robert Mansfield take charge of Rebecca Mansfield and furnish her the necessaries of life and report to the next quarterly court.

Petr Brown produced into open Court the scalp of one wild cat which he proved to the Satisfaction of the Court was killed by him in Sequatchee County. It is therefore ordered by the Court that Certificate issue to him. (Iss'd)

The Court proceeded to the election of a Sheriff occasioned by the resignation of William Rankin, and M. M. Phelps and J. C. Lockheart being the only candidates M. M. Phelps received nine votes and J. C. Lockheart received three votes. It was therefore declared that M.M. Phelps was duly and constitutionally elected Sheriff to fill the vacancy occasioned as aforesaid.

Sheriffs Bond

Know all men by these presents that we M. M. Phelps William Phelps and F. Deakins acknowledge ourselves indebted to the State of Tennessee in the sum of twelve thousand dollars to be levied of our respective goods and chattels. Lands and tenaments, Sealed with our seals and dated this 3 September 1859.

The condition of the above obligation is such that whereas the above bound M. M. Phelps was duly and constitutionally elected Sheriff of Sequatchee County to fill the vacancy occasioned by the resignation of Wm Rankin until the first Monday in April next. Now if the Said Morlin M. Phelps shall will and truly execute and due return make of all process to him P-76 directed, and pay all fees and sums of money by him recd. or levied by virtue of any process, into the proper office or to the person entitled, and faithfully to execute the office of Sheriff and perform its duties and functions during his continuance therein, then this obligation to be void otherwise to remain in full force and virtue, This day and date above written.

Approved in open Court,	M. M. Phelps	SEAL
Octr. 3rd 1859.	William Phelps	SEAL
Aaron Smith, Chm.	F. Deakins	Seal

Sheriffs Revenue Bond

Know all men by these presents that we M. M. Phelps William Phelps and F. Deakins are held and firmly bound unto the state of Tennessee in the final sum of Five hundred dollars but to be void on condition that the above bound M. M. Phelps shall faithfully collect and pay over all fines for futures & C. to the Trustee of Sequatchee County, arrising under the Act of assembly for the punishment of Small offences.

Sealed with our Seals and dated this 3rd October 1859.

Approved in open Court	M. M. Phleps	SEAL
Octr. 3rd 1859	Wm. Phelps	SEAL
Aaron Smith Chm.	F. Deakins	SEAL

Ordered by the Court that John Hatfield overseer of the public road from the Valley road across the bridge at Hatfields, have four additional hands to work on said road, to wit James Cope Pleasant Johnson Nathaniel Deakins and Franklin Johnson. (Iss'd)

Dunlap Monday October 3rd 1859.

P-77 The vote of the Court being taken on an allowance of two dollars and fifty cents to each Justice of the peace for attending this quarterly Court, to wit, G. W. Cain E. S. Owings Edwin Newby M. B. Narramore F. Deakins A. J. Tate J. C. Rickett I. N. Clark Wm B. Elliott Wm E. Kell J. M. Morrson Thomas Hicks John Odom and J. C. Lockheart. It was carried in the affirmative. It is therefore ordered by the Court that Certificate issue to them. (Iss'd)

Ordered by the Court that Peter Brown be appointed overseer of a Second class road from the top of the Hill at the corner of B. L. Bennetts lane to the top of the hill near Andersons Shop and that he have all the hands on Said Andersons farm work under him except J. Brown Rheuben Hixson and James I. Rogers. (Iss'd)

J. M. Anderson produced into Court the Scalp of one Wild cat which he proved to the Satisfaction of the Court was killed by him in Sequatchee County. It is ordered by the Court that Certificate issue to him. (Iss'd)

It is ordered by the Court that the road leading from the top of the Mountain known as the old Hill turnpike, to near A. J. Tates be reduced from a Second class to a third class road.

It is ordered by the Court that James Seals be appointed overseer of a third class road in the place of Andrew King, and that he have all the hands to work on said road that worked under former overseer. (Iss'd)

John B. Hatfield produced into open Court the Scalp of one Wild cat, which he proved to the satisfaction of the Court was killed by him in Sequatchee County. It is therefore ordered by the Court that Certificate issue to him.

P-78   Dunlap Monday, 3rd Octr 1859.

The vote of the Court being taken on an allowance of two dollars and fifty cents to Lewis Carlton for the scalp of two wild cats killed by him in Sequatchee County it was voted in the affirmative. It is therefore ordered by the Court that the Trustee pay the same out of any County moneys in his hands nototherwise appropriated and that Certificate issue to him. (Iss'd)

M. M. Phelps who was elected Shiriff appeared into open Court and took the oaths of office necessary to his qualification, and enteredupon the discharge of his duties.

W. R. Henson appeared into open Court and asked the Court to bind to him, William Harvey a minor opphan about fifteen years of age until the age of twenty one years.

The condition of said apprenticeship are as follows The

said minor is to live with the said W. R. Henosn and perform such <u>manuel</u> labor as may be required of him until he arrives to the age of twenty one years, and the said Henson is to feed and clothe him during said time, and give him schooling sufficient to enable him to cypher through the "Single rule of three" and when he has served out his minority Said Henson is to furnish him with two good suits of clothes, and a horse Bridle and Saddle to be worth seventy five dollars.

The Court also <u>requeres</u> said W. R. Henson to enter into bond in the sum of three hundred dollars with good Security, conditional for the faithful performance of Said contract, which is done accordingly, It is as follows :

Apprentice Bond of W. R. Henson.

Know all men by these presents that we W. R. Henson and John Henson are held and firmly bound unto the State of Tennessee for the use of William Harvey in the final sum of three hundred dollars, for which payment well and truly to be made, we bind ourselves our heirs & C. jointly   P-79   severally and firmly by these presents, Sealed with out Seals and dated this 3rd Octr. 1859.

The condition of the above is Such that whereas the above bound W. R. Henson has this day had a minor child, William Harvey bound to him aged about fifteen years.

Now is the Said W. R. Henson shall well and truly perform the Contract entered into between him and the County Court in relation to Said Apprentice, then this obligation to be void otherwise to remain in full force and virtue.

This day and date above, Written   W. R. Henosn   SEAL
Approved by me   John Henson   SEAL
S. C. Stone Clerk.

Ordered that Court adjourn until tomorrow morning at
8 o'clock   Aaron Smith Chm
                   M. B. Narramore
                   George W. Cain
                   W. B. Elliott
                   A. J. Tate
                   F. Deakins
                   John Odom

Court met pursuant to adjournment. Present on the bench Aaron Smith G. W. Cain M. B. Narramore William B. Elliott A. J. Tate - William Rankin and A. J. Tate administrators of the estate of A. H. Lockheart decd petitioned the Court to Sell the real estate of said Lockheart which petition is recd. and it is ordered that James Lockheart be appointed guardian Ad litum for Robert Lockheart minor heir, and the minor heirs of Prudence Dugan dec'd and that notice be served upon the heirs of said A. H. Lockheart to appear at the next term of this

Court and answer said petition and show cause if any they have why a decree should not be rendered to sell said land.

P-80   Dunlap Tuesday 4th Oc tr 1859.

There being no further buisiness it is ordered that Court adjourn until Court in Course,

Aaron Smith chm.
M. B. Narramore
W. B. Elliott

County Court, November term, 1859.
Dunlap Monday, 7th Nov. 1859.

Quorum Court met pursuant to adjournment. Present on the bench Esqrs. Aaron Smith M. B. Narramore and S. D. Thurman.

William Rankin admr of the estate of A. J. Lockheart Dec'd appeared into open Court and asked leave of the Court for further time until the next term of this Court to Sell the land of Said Lockheart, so as to give the legal notice to the heirs of Said estate which to him is granted.

James Seals produced into open Court the scalp of one wild cat, which he proved to the Satisfaction of the Court was killed by him in Sequatchee County. (Iss'd) It is therefore ordered that Certificate issue to him.

James W. Hatfield admr. of the estate of George Rogers and also the petitioned the Court to Sell the real estate of Said Rogers and also the undivided interest his heirs have in the dower of Patience Rogers dec'd. which is petition being fully understood by the Court. It is ordered that notice be served upon Susan Rogers the widow of Said George Rogers dec'd and the guardian adlitum for the minor heirs of Said George Rogers dec'd - to appear at the next term of this Court to answer said petition and show cause if any they have why Said land Should not be sold.

P-81   Dunlap Monday 7th Nov. 1859.

It is ordered by the Court that Josiah Rogers be appointed guardian Ad litum for the minor heirs of George Rogers deceased Court adjourned until Court in Course   Aaron Smith Chm.
S. D. Thurman   M. B. Narramore

Dunlap Monday. 5th Decr. 1859.

County Court met pursuant to adjournment. Present on the bench, Esqrs. Aaron Smith S. D. Thurman M. B. Narramore F. Deakins Wm E. Kell

Wm R. Deakins produced into open Court the scalp of one wild cat which he proved to the Satisfaction of the Court was killed by him in Sequatchee County. It is therefore ordered by the Court that Certificate issue to him. (Iss'd)

James W. Hatfield admr.) This cause came on to be heard
of George Rogers decd) on petition of the administra-
vs) tor, when it appeared that
Susan Rogers et al.) George Rogers died in the year
1858, seized of a tract, of land, in fee simple, lying on the East side of Sequatchee river in Sequatchee County on which he resided at the time of his death. Containing about fifty acres, also an undivided interest in the dower of Patience Rogers decd. And it appearing to the Court that the personal estate of George Rogers the plaintiff intestate amounted only to the sum of one hundred and twenty four dollars and four cents and that the debts and there still remained unpaid about one hundred and fifty dollars of debts.

P-82 Against the intestates estate, and that it is necessary and proper to Sell the land above described which decended to the defendants as heirs of Said deceased for the payment thereof.

It is therefore decreed by the Court that the Clerk of this Court proceed to Sell Said land at public Sale after giving thirty days notice at the Court house and threeother public places in Said County. He is to Sell said tract of land on a credit of Six, twelve and eighteen months in equal portions except five percent which is to be required to be paid down taking bond and security for the purchase money and the Court further decrees that the undivided interest in the dower of Patience Rogers decd. be sold on a credit of eighteen months for the use of the minorheirs of George Rogers decd. taking note and Security for the purchase money. The minimum price of the George Rogers tract is to be $300. tree hundred dollars, the interest in the dower is to start at $10 ten dollars per acre.

Ordered that Court adjourn until Court in Course,
Aaron Smith chm
S. D. Thurman
M. B. Narramore

P-83   Dunlap January 2nd 1860.

County Court met pursuant to adjournment. Present on the bench Esqrs. Aaron Smith S. D. Thurman Wm E. Kell M. B. Narramore J. M. Morrison J. C. Lockheart J. C. Rickett E. S. Owings I. N. Clark A. J. Tate F. Deakins Wm. B. Elliott George W. Cain Edwin Newby Bram Heard.

The vote of the Court being taken on an allowance of Sixteen dollars and seventy five cents to M. M. Phelps for services rendered as Shiriff of Sequatchee County. It was voted in the affirmative. It is therefore ordered by the Court that

Certificate issue to him. (Iss'd)

The vote of the Court being taken on an allowance of twenty one dollars and five cents to Robert Mansfield for keeping Rebecca Mansfield, a pauper. It was voted in the affirmative. It is therefore ordered by the Court that Certificate issue to him. (Iss'd)

The vote of the Court being taken on an allowance of fifteen dollars and thirty three cents to William Stewart for keeping Fredrick Narramore, a pauper. It was voted in the affirmative. It is therefore ordered by the Court that Certificate issue to him. (Iss'd)

The voteof the Court being taken on an allowance of seventy dollars and eighty cents to I. N. Clark for keeping John Cagle, a pauper. It was voted in the affirmative. It is therefore ordered by the Court that Certificate issue to him. (Iss'd)

The voteof the Court being taken on an allowance of three dollars and fifty cents for fourteen days making forty nine dollars to Aaron Smith for acting as Chairman of the County Court for the year 1859, those who voted in the affirmative were S. D. Thurman P-84 Wm E. Kell M. B. Narramore J. M. Morrison J. C. Lockheart J. C. Rickett A. J. Tate E. S. Owings I. N. Clark Wm B Elliott F Deakins G. W. Cain Edwin Newby Byram Heard - Negative none. It is therefore ordered by the Court that Certificate issue to him.

The vote of the Court being taken on an allowance of one dollar and fifty cents to S. D. Thurman and M. B. Narramore for acting as Associate Justices in the Quorum Court, for ten dats making fifteen dollars each and also and also two dollars and fifty cents per day to Thurman for two days as one of the Justices of the quarterly Court, It was voted in the affirmative. It is therefore ordered by the Court that Certificate issue to him. (Iss'd)

Ordered by the Court that Riley McWilliams be appointed overseer, of a Second class road in the place of Malcom Hunter, and that he have the same bounds of hands as worked under former oversee. (Iss'd)

Ordered by the Court that William Hatfield be appointed overseer of the public road in the place of Isaac Johnson, and that he have the same boundsof hands as worked under former overseer. (Iss'd)

The Court then proceeded to the election of Collector of the public taxes for the year 1869, James I. Rogers and Daswell Rogers being the candidates. Daswell Rogers received ten votes and James I. Rogers received five votes. Daswell Rogers having received the highest number of votes was declared duly elected Collector for the present year.

The vote of the Court being taken on an allowance of sixteen dollars and forty five cents to S. C. Stone Clk. for services rendered as such it was voted in the affirmative. It is therefore ordered by the Court that Certificate issue to him.

P-85   Dunlap Monday Jany 2nd 1860.

It is ordered by the Court that the <u>Shiriff</u> of Sequatchee County summons the following persons citizens of Sequatchee County, to Serve as Jurors at the April term 1860 of the Circuit Court for Said County

Dist 1st - Howard Griffin, Allen Walker, Byram Heard, A. R. Thurman
"   2nd - J. C. Rickett Jesse Savage
"   3   - Malcom Johnson, W. R. Henson, F.M. Hatfield, Isaac Johnson
"   4   - F. M. McDonough, Washington Cain, W. B. Elliott, Isaac Jones
"   5   - Thomas Bailey, John C. Lockheart, Wm E. Kell J. M. Anderson
"   6   - Robert Hoodenpyle J. C. Morrison William Marlin
"   7   - Harris Doolie David Vomen
"   8   - Littleton Cagle Charles Moffatt

Constalbes to wait on the Court Bird Clark and Caswell P. Ewton.

The Court then proceeded to elect a chairman G. W. Cain and M. B. Narramore being the Candidates G. W. Cain received eight votes and M. B. Narramore received six votes, G. W. Cain having recd the highest number of votes was duly and Constitutionally elected Chairman of the County Court of Sequatchee for the ensuing twelve months.

The vote of the Court being taken on an allowance of two dollars and fifty cents to each Justice of the peace for attending the present term of the County Court, it was voted in the affirmative. It is therefore ordered by the Court that Certificate issue to them. (Iss'd)

Wm Rankin & A J Tate admrs.)   This cause came on to be
         vs   )   heard before the worshipful
James Lockheart et al   )   County Court of Sequatchee
County, on the petition of the admrs. when it appeared that A. H. Lockheart died in the year 1858 possessed of certain tracts of land lying in Said County on the top of Cumberland Mountain adjoining the lands of Vester & Cain George W. Cain and others on which he resided at the time of his death.   P-86   Containing about 3200 hundred acres and it appearing to the Court that the proceeds of the personal property was not sufficient to satisfy the liabilities of said estate, and that it is necessary and proper to sell the land above described which <u>desended</u> to the defendants as heirs of Said estate for the payment <u>thereof</u>.

It is therefore ordered by the Court that the Clerk of this

Court proceed to sell said Land subject to dower, on a credit of twelve months except five per cent which is required to be paid down also the amt. of purchase money due to Jonathan Hatfield, after giving thirty days notice at three public places in Sequatchee County, Note and approved security will be required of the purchaser.

Mrs. Carmack, a pauper, being put up at the lowest bidder, Henrietta Griffith bid ninety cents per week for twelve months, being the lowest bidder she was let off to her for twelve months.

Mrs. Barbary Cagle and Eliza Cagle, (paupers) was cryed off by the Shiriff to the lowest bidder and E. H. Price being the lowest at 50 dollars each for twelve months they were knocked off to him for that amount.

Rebecca Mansfield (a pauper) being put up to be kept for twelve months, to the lowest bidder Norman Mansfield bid eighty seven dollars, it being the lowest bid she was let off to him for that amount.

Eleven Jones (a pauper) was be agreement of the Court to be taken charge of by Joseph Jones for 1.00 per week for twelve months.

P-37   Dunlap, Monday, January 2nd 1860.

By agreement of the Court M. B. Narramore takes charge of and furnish Fredrick & Nancy Narramore such necessaries as they may stand in need of for twelve months for the Sum of fifty two dollars.

The Court then proceeded to the election of Ranger and Alexander McDonough being the only candidate received four votes, and was therefore declared duly elected Ranger for the next two years.

The Court then went into the election of Coroner. Jonathan Hatfield received five votes being the entire vote polled - and was elected Coroner for the ensuing two years.

The Court appointed the following persons, as revenue commissioners to assess the taxes for the year 1860.

Dist					
1st	Byram Heard	-	2	A. J. Tate	
" 3	M. B. Narramore	-	4	G. W. Cain	
" 5	J. C. Lockheart	-	6	J. M. Morrison	
" 7	Edwin Newby	-	8	I. N. Clark	

Wm B. Elliott produced into open Court the scalp of one wild cat which he proved to the Satisfaction of the Court was killed by him in Sequatchee County. It is therefore ordered by the Court that Certificate issue to him.

It appearing to the Court from satisfactory proff adduced that William Dugan has been illegally taxed with a poll - It is ordered by the Court that he be relieved from paying said poll tax, and that the tax collector from collecting the same.

John C. Lockheart Collector of the public taxes for the year 1859, returned into Court the following list of delinquent tax payers.

P-88   Dunlap Monday, January 2nd 1860.

Monroe Lusk	1 poll	- 1.25	W. T. Adams	1 poll	- 1.25
Wilson Conner	1 "	- 1.25	Thomas Adams	1 "	- 1.25
Wm S. Wilson	1 "	- 1.25	Melton Caps	1 "	- 1.25
Wm Camp	1 "	- 1.25	James Connor	1 "	- 1.25
Jacob Cass	1 "	- 1.25	J. M. Richards	1 "	- 1.25
Wesley Childers	1 "	- 1.25	Wm C. Privette	1 "	- 1.25
Wilson Bornes	1 "	@ 1.25	Sam'l Fondrau	1 "	- 1.25
Champ Ramsey	1 "	- 1.25	Houston Hall		1.35
Joseph Ables	1 "	- 1.25	Williamson Heard		1.25
David Ables	1 "	- 1.25	James C. Mickle		1.25
Levi Fairbanks	1 "	- 1.25	Thomas Green		2.50
Peyton Christian	1 "	- 1.25	John Hoodenpyl		2.57
			John Odom		1.25
State of Tennessee)			Anderson Cannon		1.25
Sequatchee County)			Wm. Dugan		1.25
					36.56

I, John C. Lockheart collector of the public taxes for the year 1859, do certify that the above is a ture statement of the delinquent taxpayers which I was unable to collect.
                                    John C. Lockheart Collector

It is therefore ordered by the Court that said Lockheart as collector aforesaid be released from paying said amt of thirty six dollars and fifty six cents.

The Court appointed the following persons to lay the tax on property polls and privaliges - Wm B. Elliott E. S. Owings and J. C. Rickett for the year 1860, which is as follows-
  On real estate and personal property 26 per cent
  On polls   1.00
  On Privaliges   same as state tax
  On Pauper tax
  On real and personal property   10 per cent
  On polls   50 cents
                              Wm B. Elliott
                              J. C. Rickett
                              E. S. Owings

Which report of Com. being fully understood by the Court is in all things is in all things confirmed.

P-89   Dunlap Monday January 2nd 1860.

The Court then proceeded to ballot for two Justices to act

with the chairman as a quorem Court and Wm B. Elliott and J. C. Lockheart received the highest number of votes and was therefore elected.

    Court adjourned until tomorrow morning at 8 o'clock
                George W. Cain chairman
                Wm B. Elliott
                J. M. Morrison
                J. C. Lockheart
                M. B. Narramore

    Court met pursuant to adjournment. Present G. W. Cain Wm B. Elliott J. C. Lockheart M. B. Narramore J.M. Morrison.

    Wm Rankin and others petitioned the Court for the _privalige_ of building a free bridge across Sequatchee river at the point designated by a report of a Jury of view, to locate a road from Dunlap across the river to the east side of Sequatchee valley and also to appoint five commissioners to superintend the construction, of Said bridge, which petition being fully understood by the Court is granted to them. and the Court appointed J. H. Rogers B. B. Cannon Jo R. Brown Wm B. Elliott & G. W. Cain - as said Commissioners.

    The Court appointed the following persons to act as Judges of an election to be held on the first Saturday in March next for the purpose of acting County and district officers - to wit,
Dist. 1st - A. R. Thurman Thomas Minton John McWilliams
     2 - A. J. Tate Jesse Savage Gilbert Hatfield
     3 - William Stewart James Jones Jerry Hatfield
     4 - Wm B. Elliott James Mansfield James Hatifield
     5 - Joshua Easterly B. S. Bennett Thos. J. Hoodenpyl
     6 - Eph Thurman Austin Hackworth Albert Saunders
P-90 7 - Aaron Brimer Sampson Brock John Pickett
     8 - E. S. Owings I. N. Clark Thomas King

    There being no further _buisiness_ the Court adjourned until Court in Course
                            George W. Cain Chairman
                            W. B. Elliott
                            J. C. Lockheart

    Dunlap Monday Feb. 6th 1860

    County Court met pursuant to adjournment. Present on the bench the worshipful chairman G. W. Cain Wm B. Elliott M. B. Narramore S. D. Thurman Wm E. Kell J. M. Morrison F. Deakins John C. Lockheart

    Ordered by the Court that Isaac Williams be appointed overseer of a Second class road from the Stage road to the opposite valley road crossing Sequatchee river at Hatfield bridge, and to have the following hands to work on said road- All the hands on the home farm of George Stewart F. J. Johnson James W. Hatfield Margaret Deakins Isaac Williams Jonathan Hatfield on the west side of Sequatchee Valley. (Iss'd)

Ordered by the Court that John Hughes be appointed overseer of a first class road in the place of John Teaters, and that he have the same bounds of hands as worked under former overseer.

John Henson who was appointed guardian for the minor heirs of James Heard at the Junes session of this Court tenders his resignation as guardian aforesaid and thereupon the Court appointed John H. Rogers guardian for said minors in his stead

P-91   Dunlap, Monday Feb. 6th 1860

John H. Rogers who was appointed guardian for the minor heirs of James Heard decd appeared into open Court and entered into bond with D J Rogers J M Anderson F Deakins as his security in the sum of five thousand dollars for the faithful performance of his duties and also took the oath necessary to his qualification.

Bond ordered to be recorded. It is ordered by the Court that E. S. Owings be appointed guardian for Charles N. Owings minor heirs of John Owings decd.

E. S. Owings who was appointed guardian for Charles N. Owings appeared into Court and gave his bond in the Sum of three hundred dollars with Wm B. Elliott as his Security - for the faithful performance of his duty as such guardian and was qualified according to law. Bond ordered to be recorded.

Information having been given to the Court that Charlotte Loven a female orphan child is destitute and without a proper home. It is ordered therefore by the Court that the Sheriff of Sequatchee County take charge of Said child and bring her up to the next County Court to be disposed of according to law.

Ordered by the Court that Joseph Abson be appointed overseer of a Second class road in the place of B. L. Bennett and that he have the same bounds of hands as worked under former overseer. (Iss'd)

Ordered by the Court that Overton Dille be appointed overseer of a Second class road in the place of Jonathan Turner, and that he have the same bounds of hands as worked under former overseer.

Ordered that Court adjourn until Court in Course
George W. Cain   Chairman
W. B. Elliott
John C. Lockheart

P-92   Dunlap Monday March 5th 1860.

Quorum Court met on the first Monday in March 1860 for the purpose of transacting such County buisiness as may come before it Present on the bench the worshipful Chairman, J. C.

Lockheart Wm B. Elliott and other Justices.

James B. Smith petitioned the Court to grant him the privalige of changing the public road, near his house commencing west of his house, and near it running east course about thirty yards form the old road and intersecting the Same on the Side of the hill, the whole distance being about two hundred yards - which privalige was granted him, by his making the new road as good as the old before changing the same.

Ordered by the Court that Elias McCarver be appointed overseer of a third class road from the old Marion County line to the Peyton Christian place and that he have all the hands to work on Said road that formally worked under the old overseer. (Iss'd)

Ordered by the Court that B. B. Cannon be appointed overseer of a Second class road in the place of C. L. Lewis and that he have the Same bounds of hands as worked under former overseer. (Iss'd)

It is ordered by the Court that Albert Saunders overseer of public road have the hands on Jesse Picketts home farm work under him. (Iss'd)

Sam'l Brown having presented to the Court a complete transcript of his guardianship of the minor heirs of Malcom Johnson Decd. from the County Court of Marion County and the Court being satisfied that the proceedings were regular - he was appointed guardianship for Said minors by this Court, and the Clerk was ordered to record said transcript.

Sam'l McBroom who was appointed guardian for the minor heirs of Malcom Johnson Decd appeared P-93 into Court and gave a bond the penalty of which was one thousand dollars, with F; J. Johnson as his Security, which was approved by the Court and took an oath to discharge his duty according to law.

It is ordered by the Court that Burrel Barker overseer of the public road have two additional hands to work under him on his Section of the road, to wit, William Fredricks and Hezekiah Harvey - (Iss'd)

John H. Rogers who was appointed guardian for the minor heirs of James Heard decd at the Feb. term of this Court appeared into Court, and rendered a Statement of the amount of his wards property - which was ordered by the Court to be recorded in the guardian book.

Ordered that Court adjourn until Court in Course
George W. Cain Chairman
W. B. Elliott

Dunlap, Monday, 2nd April 1860.

County Court met pursuant to adjournment, Present on the

bench the worshipful chairman G. W. Cain William B. Elliott
Aaron B. Smith M. B. Narramore S. D. Thurman Wm D. Kell
J. C. Lockheart J. M. Morrison William M. Bennett A. J. Tate
J. C. Rickett E. S. Owings I. N. Clark

Franklin Deakins who was elected Clerk of the County Court of Sequatchee County presented to the Court a Certificate of his election, and entered into bonds which was approved by the Court, and took the oaths necessary to his qualification.

P-94   Dunlap, Monday April 2nd 1860.
         County Court Clerk's Official Bond.

Know all men by these presents that we F. Deakins F. J. Johnson Madison Deakins and S. D. Thurman acknowledge ourselves indebted to the State of Tennessee in the Sum of two thousand dollars, which payment well and truly to be made, we bind ourselves and each of us jointly & Severally by these presents. Sealed with our Seals and dated this 2nd day of April 1860.

The condition of the above obligation is such that whereas the above bound F. Deakins was on the 3rd day of March 1860 duly and constitutionally elected Clerk of the County Court of Sequatchee County for the ensuing four years, and until his Successor is chosen and qualified.

Now is the said F. Deakins shall faithfully keep the records of his office, and perform its duties, then this obligation shall be void otherwise to remain in full force & effect,

Witness our hands and Seals, this day and date above written
Approved by the Court   F. Deakins   SEAL
    April 2nd 1860   F. J. Johnson   SEAL
        George W. Cain, Chm.   Madison Deakins   SEAL
                                    S. D. Thurman   SEAL

County Clerks Revenue Bond.

Know all men by these presents that we Franklin Deakins F. J. Johnson Madison Deakins and S. D. Thurman acknowledge ourselves indebted to the State of Tennessee in the sum of five thousand dollars, for which payment we bind ourselves jointly and severally. Sealed with our seals and dated this 2nd April 1860.

The conditional the above obligation is such that whereas the above bound F. Deakins was on the 3rd day of March 1860 duly elected clerk of the County Court of Sequatchee County for the ensuing four years, and until his successore is qualified.

P-95 Now if the Said F. Deakins shall faithfully account for and apy over all moneys arising from taxes and suits fines and forfeitures, then this obligation to be void, otherwise remain in full force and virtue, Witness our hands and Seals.
    This day and date above written,   F. Deakins   SEAL
    Approved by the Court   F. J. Johnson   SEAL
      April 2nd 1860   Madison Deakins   SEAL
        George W. Cain, chm.   S. D. Thurman   SEAL

Aaron Smith George W. Cain Wm M. Bennett Simpson Brock, F. M. McDonough Justices of the Peace who were elected on the 3rd day of March 1860 and who were elected have been commissioned by the Governor appeared into open Court, gave their bonds with approved security and took the oaths necessary to their qualifications.

A vacancy having occurred in the office of chairman of the County Court. George W. Cain was reelected chairman of the County Court upon the first ballot.

It appearing to the Satisfaction of the Court that Jonathan Pope has departed this life intestate and also that Thomas A. Pope and William Rankin are entitled to the administration, It is therefore ordered by the Court that they be appointed administrators as aforesaid.

It is ordered by the Court that the order heretofore made by this Court declaring Rebecca Mansfield a pauper be recinded.

The order of the Court heretofore made declaring Mrs. Carmack a pauper is hereby recinded.

P-96 The vote of the Court being taken on an allowance to Henritta Griffith of Ninety Cents per week for nine weeks, for keeping Mrs. Carmack a pauper, making in all eight dollars and ten cents. It was voted in the affirmative.

The vote of the Court being taken on an allowance of ten dollars to Norman Mansfield for keeping Rebecca Mansfield a pauper six weeks it was voted in the affirmative.

An order heretofore made by the Court declaring Louise Cagle a pauper, is hereby recinded.

Information having been given to the Court that the property belonging to a minor heir of S. J. A. Burg, is going to waste, & C, It is ordered by the Court, that David Brown and David Varner be appointed Commissioners to examine into the condition of said property and child, and report to the next term of this Court.

Madison Deakins guardian for Elizabeth McLain minor heir of Daniel McLain deceased reported to the Court the amount of proceeds which have come into his hands as such guardian and also the disbursements made by him - which the Court ordered to be recorded in the guardian book.

William Johnson who was elected Sheriff of Sequatchee County on the 3rd day of March 1860 presented to the Court a Certificate of his election, and gave his bonds with approved Security, and took the oaths necessary to his qualification.

P-97   Dunlap Monday 2nd April 1860.

Sheriff's Official Bond.

Know all men by these presents that we Wm Johnson F. Deakins F. J. Johnson and Sam'l Brown acknowledge ourselves indebted to the State of Tennessee in the Sum of twelve thousand dollars which payment well and truly to be made, we bind ourselves and each of us jointly severally and firmly by these presents. Sealed with our Seals and dated 2nd day of April 1860.

The condition of the above obligation is such that whereas the above named William Johnson duly and Constitutionally elected Sheriff of Sequatchee County by the qualified voters of said County on the 3rd day of March 1860 for two years.

Now is the Said William Johnson shall well and truly execute and due return make of all precepts to him directed and to pay all fees and somes of money by him rreceived or levied by return of any process into the proper office or to the person entitled and faithfully Execute the office of Sheriff and perform its duties and functions during his continuance therein then the above obligation to be void otherwise to remain in full force and Effect. Witness our hands and seqls this day and date above written

Approved by the Court		
April 2nd 1860	William Johnson	SEAL
G. W. Cain Chm.	F. Deakins	SEAL
	F. J. Johnson	SEAL
	Samuel Brown	SEAL

Sheriff's Revenue Bond.

Know all men by these presents that we William Johnson F. Deakins F. J. Johnson Samuel McBrown William Heard William Rankin acknowledge ourselves to be indebted to the State of Tennessee in the Some of five hundred dollars to be void on condition that the said William Johnson who was elected Sheriff of P-98 the County of Sequatchee, Tennessee on the 3rd day of March 1860, shall faithfully collect and pay over to the Trustee of Sequatchee County, all fines and forfeitures which he ought to collect and pay over under the Small offence law passed by the general assembly of Tennessee, then this obligation to be void otherwise to remain in full force and effect, This 2nd day of April 1860.

Approved by the Court	William Johnson	SEAL
April 2nd 1860	F. Deakins	SEAL
G. W. Cain. Chm.	F.J. Johnson	SEAL
	Samuel Brown	SEAL
	William Heard	SEAL
	William Rankin	SEAL

Oliver M. Hatfield asked the Court to bind to him Charlotte Samples, a minor orphand child aged about fourteen years until she arrives at the age of eighteen years - which the Court is pleased to do upon the following conditions, Said Hatfield is to find and provide for her diet, cloths lodgings and accomadations fit and necessary - and shall teach or cause her her to be taught to read and write and cypher as far as the rule of three - and for the faithful performance of Said contract the Court has required Said Hatfield to enter into bond with Security in the Sum of two hundred & fifty dollars which bond is in the following words & figures, to wit,

Apprentice Bond

State of Tennessee) Wee Oliver M. Hatfield &
Sequatchee County) F. M. McDonough
acknowledge ourselves indebted to the State of Tennessee for this use of within named orpen childe in the Sums of Two hundred &fifty dollars but to be void on condition that the Said O. M. Hatfield has this day had Charlotte Samples an orphen child bound to him ontill she arivs at the age of Eighteen years well faithfully and ovestely discharge all his duties to said P-99 chld and well and truly comply with the contract by him maid with Court then this obligation to be void otherwise to remain in full force and Effect Witnessour hands and seals this 2nd day of April 1860

  Approved by the Court   O. M. Hatfield   SEAL
   George W Cain   F. M. McDonough   SEAL
    Charman

 Aaron Brimer petitioned the Court to have Mary Elizabeth Porter a minor orphan child about six years of age bound to him until she arrives at the age of eighteen years which the Court orders to be done, upon the following conditions - that is to say - the said Aaron Brimer is to find and provide for her, diet clothes lodging and accomodations fit and necessary and shall teach or cause to be taught to her, to read and write and bypher to the rule of three, for the performance of which contract the Court has required said Brimer to enter into bond with Security in the sum of two hundred & fifty dollars - The following is said bond.

Apprentice Bond.

 Know all men by these presents that we Aaron Brimer and Simpson Brock acknowledge our Selves indebted to the State of Tennessee in the sum of two hundred and fifty dollars for the use of the within named orphan But to be void on Condition that the Said Aaron Brimer who has this day had Mary E. Porter an opphan child bound to him until the age of eighteen years, who is now about Six years old Shall well and truly comply with the contract by him made with the County Court, and faithfully and honestly to discharge all the duties to said child - Witness our hands and seals, this 2nd day of April 1860

  Approved in Court   Aaron Brimer   SEAL
  2nd April 1860   Simpson Brock   SEAL
  G. W. Cain Chm.

P-100   Dunlap Monday, 2nd April 1860.

 It is ordered by the Court that the Sheriff open and hold an election after giving lawful notice for one Justice of the Peace and one Constable in the first Civil district of Sequatchee County.

Ordered by the Court that E. T. Sawyers be appointed overseer of the public road Second class in the place of James Mansfield, and that he have the Same bounds of hands as worked under former overseer. (Iss'd)

Ordered by the Court that M. E. Deakins be appointed overseer of a first class road in place of J. C. Wimberly and that he have the Same bounds of hands as worked under former overseer. (Iss'd)

Jesse Pickett produced into open Court the Scalp of one wild cat Scalp which he proved to the Satisfaction of the Court was killed by him in Sequatchee County. It is therefore ordered by the Court that Certificate issue to him. (Iss'd)

Isaac Hicks who was appointed Deputy Shff appeared into Court and gave his bond and took the oaths necessary to his qualification.

Samuel McBrown who was elected Trustee of Sequatchee County, on the 3rd day of March 1860, appeared into Court, and gave his bonds required by law, with approved Security - and took the oaths necessary to his qualification.

Trustees Bond
Common School funds

Know all men by these presents that we Saml. McBrown James M. Stewart F. J. Johnson & George Stewart, acknowledged ourselves indebted to the State of Tennessee in the Sum of P-101 fifteen hundred dollars Sealed with ourselves and dated this 2nd April 1860.

The condition of this obligation is Such that Whare as Samuel McBrown was duly Elected Trustee of Sequatchee County for the ensuing two years and ontill his Successor is qualified.

Now if the Said Samuel Brown Shall faithfully pay over according to law all moneys which may come into his hands on account of Comon Scools then this obligation to be void otherwise to remain in full force and virtue

Approved by the Court	Samuel McBrown	SEAL
George W. Cain	F. J. Johnson	SEAL
Chairman	George Stewart	SEAL

Trustees official Bond.

Know all men by these presents that we Samuel McBrown James M. Stewart F. J. Johnson George Stewart acknolledge ourselves indebted to this State of Tennessee in the penal Some of two thousand dollars Sealed with out Seals and dated this 2 day of April 1860

The condition of the above obligation is such that whare as the above bonden Samuel McBrown was on the 3rd day of March 1860 duly Elected Trustee for the Sequatchee County for the ensuing two years and ontill his successor is qualified. If

therefore the Said Samuel McBrown Shall Safely keepe and
faithfully pay all moneys deposited in his hands agreeably
to have and the order of the Court Then this obligation to
be void otherwise to remain in full force and effect.

           Samuel McBrown SEAL
 Approved by the Court James M. Stewart SEAL
 April 2nd 1860   F. J. Johnson SEAL
 G.W. Cain Chm.   George Stewart SEAL

P-102   Dunlap Monday 2nd April 1860
    Small Offence Bond

Know all men by these presents that we Samuel McBrown
James M. Stewart F. J. Johnson George Stewart acknowledged
our selvs indebted to the State of Tennessee in the some of
Twenty five hundred dollars sealed with our seals and dated
this 2nd day of April 1860 The condition of the above obligation is such that whereas the said Samuel M. C. Brown is
Trustee of Sequatchee County now if said Trustee shall faithfully account for all moneys received by him ariseing under
the act for the punishment of small offices and faithfully
discharge the duties as Trustee in the behalf, then this
obligation to be void otherwise to remain in full force and
Effect. Witness our hands and seals

 Approved by the Court Samuel McBrown SEAL
  April 2nd 1860   James M. Stewart SEAL
   George W. Cain Chm. F. J. Johnson   SEAL
           George Stewart SEAL

  J. C. Wimberly who was elected Register for Sequatchee
County on the 3rd day of March 1860, produced to the Court
a Certificate of his electeon, and gave his bond required by
law and took the oath necessary to his qualification.

         Registers Bond.

Know all men by these presents that we J. C. Wimberly
Madison Deakins Wm M. Bennett M. M. Phelps acknowledge ourselves indebted to the state of Tennessee in the penal sum
of twelve thousand five hundred dollars.

  The condition of the above obligation is such that whereas
the above bounden J. C. Wimberly was duly and constitutionally
elected Register for the County of Sequatchee Tennessee on the
3rd day of March 1860 by the qualified voters of said County
for the ensuing four years.

P-103 If therefore the said J. C. Wimberly shall well and
truly perform all the duties required of him in Said office
according to law, then this obligation to be void otherwise to
remain in full force and effect

  This 2nd day of April 1860 J. C. Wimberly SEAL
  Approved by the Court   Madison Deakins SEAL
   April 2nd 1860   Wm. M. Bennett SEAL
    G. W. Cain, chm.   M. M. Pehlps   SEAL

  The vote of the Court being taken on an allowance of five

72.

dollars and fifty cents to S. C. Stone for services rendered as Clerk of the County Court from January until April 1860 It was voted in the affirmative.

The vote of the Court being taken on an allowance of Seventy five cents to B. B. Cannon for a record book furnished by him in the discharge of his official duties. It was voted in the affirmative.

The vote of the Court being taken on an allowance of six dollars to each revenue com. for taking down a list of the taxable property in their respective districts, to wit, 1st Byram Heard - 2nd A. J. Tate 3rd M. B. Narramore - 4th George W. Cain - 5th J. C. Lockheart 6th J. M. Morrison - 7th Edwin Newby - 8th I. N. Clark. It was voted in the affirmtive.

It is ordered by the Court that Wm B. Elliott and Aaron Smith be appointed coms. to settle with the Trustee.

Jacob Lewis, Peter Brown O. M. Hatfield who were elected Constables for their respective districts appeared into open Court and gave their bonds with approved security, and took the oaths necessary to their qualifications as constables aforesaid.

P-104 The vote of the Court being taken on an allowance of fourteen dollars and twenty five cents to M. M. Phelps for services rendered as Sheriff of Sequatchee County. It was voted in the affirmative.

Ordered by the Court that Jehu Gray be appointed overseer of the public road in the place of or on the same road that Peter T. Rankin was former overseer, and to have the same bound of hands as worked under former overseer. (Iss'd)

It was ordered by the Court that Elijah Austin Ephraim Welch & John McWilliams be appointed Judges of an election in the first Civil district for Justices of the Peace & Constable.

The vote of the Court being taken on an allowance of three dollars and eighty seven cents to O. M. Hatfield for necessaries furnished Charlotte Samples an orphan child, as per order of the Court - It was voted in the affirmative.

The vote of the Court being taken on an allowance of two dollars and fifty cents to each Justice of the Peace for serving at the present quarterly Court, to wit, A. J. Tate J. C. Rickett S. D. Thurman M. B. Narramore W. B. Elliott F. M. McDonough J. C. Lockheart Wm D. Kell Wm M. Bennett J. M. Morrison Edwin Newby Simpson Brock I. N. Clark E. S. Owings Byram Heard. It was voted in the affirmative.

Ordered that Court adjourn until 8 o'clock tomorrow morning.
George W. Cain chairman

W. B. Elliott
F. Ml McDonough
J. C. Lockheart
M. J. Morrison
Simpson Brock
Edwin Newby

P-105   Dunlap Tuesday 3rd April 1860

Court met pursuant to adjournment, Presnet on the bench George W. Cain, Wm B. Elliott J. C. Lockheart J. M. MCDonough J. M. Morrison Simpson Brock and Edwin Newby.

It is ordered by the Court that William Rankin George W. Cain and Wm B. Elliott Joseph Brown and A. B. Ewton be appointed a Jury of view, to review a road formally located by the County Court, running with the main Street of Dunlap, and intersecting the main road near the first mile poast and report to the next Court, whether it would be more practicable to change the location of Said road and to what point.

John C, Lockheart who was elected collector of Public revinue for the County of Sequatchee on the 3 day of March 1860 for the ensuing two years presented to the Court a certificate of his Election and gave his bond with approved Security and took the necessary oath for his qualification.

Collector of Public revenue Bond.

Know all men by these presents that we John Cl Lockheart Joshua Easterly & Jesse Pickett are held and firmly bound on to the State of Tennessee in the some of fifteen hundred dollars for which some we binde our selvs jointly and severally by thes presants sealed with our seals and dated 3rd day Aprial 1860

The condition of the above obligation is such that whareas the above bond J. C. Lockhart was Elected tax collector of the public revinue of Sequatchee County for the year 1860. Now if the said J. C. Lockhart shall faithfully collect and pay over to State Treasure of Tennessee all the State tax for the County of Sequatchee collected by the firste of december 1860 then this obligation to be void otherwise to remain in full foce and virtue this 3rd day of Aprial 1860.

Approved by the Court	John C. Lockhart	SEAL
April 3rd 1860	Joshua Easterly	SEAL
G. W. Cain, chm.	his Jessa x Pickett mark	SEAL

Collector County Revenue Bond.

Know all men by these presents that we J. C. Lockhart Joshua Easterly & Jesse Pickett are held and firmly bound unto the State of Tennessee in the some of fifteen hundred dollars for which some we bind our selvs by these presats sealed with our seal and dated the 3rd day of Aprial 1860. The condition of the above bonden J. C. Lockhart was Elected collector of Public revinue for Sequatchee County for the year 1860.

Now if the said J. C. Lockhart shall faithfully collect and pay over to the trustee of Sequatchee County all county Tax by him collected or which ought to be collected against the laste day of december 1860 then this obligation to be void otherwise to remain in full force and Effect this day and date above written

    Approved by the Court   John Lockhart   SEAL
      April 3rd 1860   Joshua Easterly SEAL
        George W. Cain Chm.   Jessa Pickett   SEAL

George W. Cain Chm.

J. C. Lockhart tax collector of the County of Sequatchee appeared into open Court and asked further time until the next quarterly Court to collect and pay over the County tax due which is granted to him.

There being no further buisiness Court adjourned until Court in Course.

        George W. Cain chm.
        John C. Lockhart
        W. B. Elliott
        J. M. Morrison

P-107   Dunlap Monday 7th May 1860

County Court met persuant to Adjournment present on the bench the worshipful Chairman G. W. Cain W. B. Elliott J. M. Morrison

Ordered by the Court that William Rankin & T. A. Pope as administrators of the estate of Jonathan Pope deceast aste further time to reporte on tell the nexte quarterly term of the Court as Administrators of the Estate of said deceaste which was granted

No further Buisiness the Adjourned until Court in Cours

It is ordered by the Court that the Sheriff of Sequatchee County to Summons the folloing persons Sitizens of Sequatchee County to serve as Jurors at the Aug. term of the 1860 Circuit Court for said County.

Dist 1 - Howear Griffin Allen Walker Byram Heard A. R. Thurman
" 2nd J. C. Rickett Jessa Savage
" 3 Melcom Johnson W. R. Henson F. Hatfield
" 4th F. M. McDonough Washington Cain W. B. Elliott Isaac Johnson
" 5th Thomas Bayley J. C. Lockhart W. E. Kell T. J. Hoodenpyl Robert Hodenpyl J. C. Morrison
" 6th William Marler Simpson Brock David Varner
" 7th Little Cagle Charles Moffat

Dist 8   Constables to wait on the Court C. P. Ewton
            James Davis

There being no further Business Court adjourned ontell Court in Cours

        George W. Cian Churman
        W. B. Elliott
        J. M. Morrison

Dunlap Monday June 4th 1860

County Court met persuant to adjournment presant on the bench the worshipful Charman G. W. Can W. B. Elliott Byram Heard M. B. Narramore F. M. McDonough.

P-108 William Rankin and Thomas A. Pope Administrators of the estate of Jonathan Pope dec. returns in to Court an inventory of said Estate duly certified which being fully understood by the Court is ordered to be recorded.

Thare Being no further Busness court adjourned ontell Court in Cours

        George W. Cain Chm
        Byram Heard
        W. B. Elliott

Dunlap Monday July 2nd 1860.

County Court met persuant to adjournment present on the Bench the worshipful churman G. W. Cain William B. Elliott John C. Lockhart Aron Smith Byram Heard A. J. Tate M. B. Narramore S. D. Thurman F. M. McDonough William E. Kell J. M. Morrison William M. Bennett Simpson Brock Il N. Clark.

The vote of the Court being taken on an allowance of ten dollars and fifty cents to William Johnson, for Services rendered as Sheriff of Sequatchee County, it was voted in the affirmative it is therefore Ordered by the Court that Certificate ishue (Isd)

The vote of the Court being taken on an allowance of thirty nine dollars and seventy cents to F. Deakins as Clerk of Sequatchee County it was voted in the affirmative it is therefore ordered by the Court that Certificate ishue (Isd)

Ordered by the Court that a jury of view be appointed to view and mark a road leaving the valley road at or near Thomas Pankey's big gate crossing the dry Creek at or near James Deakins to intersect the McMinville and Chattanooga, turnpike on the South side of Cumberland P-109 Mountain and That Thomas Pankey, James Deakins J. M. Morrison J. L. Stone, and Edward Pickett be appointed a jury of view and report to the next quarterly term of this Court

 S. D. Thurman tenders his resignation as justice of the

peace of the 3rd Civil District which was accepted by the cour

Ordered by the Court that S. W. Robeson A. B. Eweton and Byram Heard, be appointed commissioners to value the land and Slaves of the Estate of Jonathan Pope Deceased and report to next term of the Court

John Kell produced into open Court the Scalp of one wild cat which he proved to the Satisfaction of the Court was killed by him in Sequatchee County. It is therefore ordered by the Court that Certificate ishue to him (Isd)

Ordered by the Court that the fourth Civil District of Sequatchee County be divided into three Scolastic districts viz: We the undersigned common School Commissioners for the mutual benefit of common School Scholars in the fourth Schlastic District divide it into three districts the fourth district Shall be bounded as follows, Commencing near J. H. Hatfield's, and running eastwardly to the river so as to include said hatfield and Isaac Williams, and from near S. C. Stones, eastwardly to the river so as to include Said Stone, and William Johnson, the twelfth district to contain all the teritory north of last named line the following belong to the fourth district the thirteenth district to contain all the teritory South of the line first mentioned which formaly belonged to said fourth Scholastic district in Sequatchee County   G. W. Cain
Joseph R. Brown
M. M. Phelps Com.

P-110   Dunlap Monday July 2nd 1860.

Ordered by the Court that William B. Elliott and Madison Deakins be appointed Trustees of Rankin Academy, to fill the vacancies occasioned by the resignation of S. D. Thurman & F. Deakins,

E. H. Price Surrenders up to the Court Barbary Cagle, formaly a pauper of Sequatchee County.

The vote of the Court being taken on an allowance to each justice of the peace for there Services at this term of the Court, two dollars and fifty cents each viz: M. B. Narramore, William B. Elliott F. N. McDonough, John C. Lockhart, William E. Kell, William M. Bennett, J. M. Morrison, Simpson Brock, I. N. Clark, and Byram Heard. It is therefore ordered by the Court that Certificate ishue to them. (Isd)

Ordered by the Court that F. M. McDonough be appointed one of Quorem in place of John C. Lockhart.

Ordered by the Court that Jackson Smith, take charge of Barbary Cagle, a pauper and report to the next quarterly term term of the Court, but to have no pay for his services if the County be disorganized.

Byram Heard, Justice of the peace who was elected on the 21st day of April 1860, and who has been commissioned by the govenore appeared into open Court and gave his bond with approved Security and took the oath necessary to his qualifications.

C. P. Ewotn who was elected Constable for the first civil district of Sequatchee County appeared into open Court and gave his bond with approved Security and took the oath necessary to his qualification.

T. A. Pope, J. J. Pope) Petition to Sell land and slaves
William Rankin and others)
vs) This day came the complainants
C. V. Ranes, L.M.T. Pope) and on there motion and it
N. M. Pope and others) appearing to the Court from the Alegations in P-111 the petition sworn to by the Complainant that five of the defendants are miners viz: Lergy Vaught, Jonathan P. Vaught, Leon Frank Vaught, Dlila Jane Vaught and Byran L. Pope, and have no regular guardian it is ordered by the Court that J. R. Brown be and he is hereby appointed guardian and litom to defend the suit for Said miners it further appearing from said petition that six of the defendants viz. C. B. Ranes, Mary A. Ranes, L. M. T. Pope, N. M. Pope, Lery Vaught and Jonathan P. Vaught are nonresidents, it is further ordered that the Clerk of this Court make publication as to Said nonresident defendats requireing them to appear and answer as required by law at the next term of this Court it is futher ordered that Subponias and copys of this petition ishue and be Served on the resident defendants Viz. Delila and Leon Vaught, Byram L. Pope, and Joseph R. Brown guardian and litem to Said miners. returnable to the next term of this Court

Court adjourned until nine o'clock tomorrow morning.
George W. Cain Churman
F. M. McDonough
John C. Lockhart
W. B. Elliott
Simpson Brock

Dunlap Tuesday July 1860

Court met pursuant to adjournment. Present G. W. Cain W. B. Elliott F. M. McDonough & Simpson Brock

Ordered by the Court that the Steam mill Compamy Be released of fifteen hundred dollars & that the Tax collector releace the same

On motion of F. Deakins clerk of this Court S. C. S⁴one was appointed deputy clerk and took the oath necessary to his qualification.

Ordered that Court adjourn until Court in Course
George W. Cain Churman
W. B. Elliott
F.M. McDonoggh

P-112   Dunlap Monday, Aug. 6th 1860.

County Court met pursuant to adjournment., Present on the bench the worshipful G. W. Cain Chairman, William B. Elliott and F. M. McDonough.

The following were the proceedings

Wm Rankin Minerva Rankin) This day came the Complaim-
T. A. Pope J. J. Pope & others) ants by their attorney and
vs) mooved the Court for Judge-
C. B. Ranes Leroy Pope) ment for confessed against
M. M. Pope & others) the defendants who have not
answered. And it appearing to the Court that publication had been in the Chattanooga Advertiser for 30 days and upwards requiring the defts. who are alleged to be non-residents to wit Thos. B. Rains Mary A. Rains, Leroy M. L. Pope, Napoleon M. Pope Leroy Vaught and Jonathan P. Vaught to appear on or before the first Monday of August 1860, and answer the complainants bill, and that said defendants have faith to appear and answer, as required, it is further ordered that the Complainants bill be taken for confessed as to said defendants and set for hearing exparte as to them.

William Rankin Minerva Rankin) Be it remembered that
Thos. A. Pope J. J. Pope Benj Hawkins) this cause came on to
Delila J. Hawkins vs) be heard on this the
Charles B Rains Mary A. Rains) 6th day of August 1860
Leroy M. L. Pope N. M. Pope, Leroy) before the Justices
Vaught Leon Vaught, Delila Vaught) of the County Court
Byram L. Pope, and J. R. Brown) of Sequatchee County
guardian ad litum) on the Complainants
bill taken for confessed as against the defendants C. B. Rains Mary A. Rains Leroy M. L. Pope N. M. Pope Leroy Vaught Jonathan P. Vaught and the answers of Leroy Vaught Jonathan P. Vaught and the Delila Vaught and Byran L. Pope minors, by their guardian, Joseph R. Brown and the proof in the cause, When it appeared to the Court that Jonathan Pope departed this life intestate in the County of Sequatchee, and State of Tennessee   P-113 on the 17th day of March 1860 that the complainants William Rankin, and Thomas A. Pope were regularly appointed admrs. on said estate and entered upon their duties as required by law, that there is ample means outside of the land and slaves belonging to said estate, to pay all the outstanding debts that the intestate left a widow that she survived him but two days and died, that he left the complainants and defendants except J. R. Brown, his only heirs and distributes, that he also left four negroes to wit Harvey Addison Ann and Lot, that he also left three tracts of land lying in Sequatchee County, or the greater part lying in Sequatchee, and the ballance in Bledsoe County. Then adjoining each other, and lying on Sequatchee River adjoining the lands of Thomas A. Pope, on the north Joseph Minton on the West, Aaron Hughs on the sough and Joseph Hixson and John McWilliams on the east, containing about seven hundred acres, more or less, and being the same lands and farm, on which the

said decd. resided at the time of his death, it further appears that five of the defendants are minors, that process has been duly executed on Leon Vaught Delila Vaught Byran L. Pope three of said minors and that Leroy Vaught and Jonathan P. Vaught the other two minors are non-residents, and that publication has been duly made against them and that Joseph R. Brown hasheretofore been duly appointed by the Court guardian ad litum for all of said minors, that process has been served on him as such and that he has answered the Complainants bill for such minors. It further appears that the Complainant are desirous that said slaves and land should be partitioned or divided amongst the several heirs and distributes and pray for a sale of said land and slaves and a division of the proceeds, But because the Court is not Satisfied whether said land and slaves can be partitioned amongst said distributees or whether it is for the interest of the several distributees that said land and slaves should be sold and the proceeds divided - It is ordered and decreed that the Clerk of this Court take <u>proff</u> and report to the present term of this Court as to the practibility and propriety of selling said land and slaves.

P-114 And said cause coming on again to be heard upon the report of the Clerk of this Court ordered at the present term, and Said report being unexcepted to, is hereby in all things confirmed. From which it appears that the estate of the decd. should be divided into new shares, that the four negroes cannot be partitioned, and that the land is not <u>susseptible</u> of and equal partition, and that it is manifestly for the interest of all the heirs and distributees of Said estate, that said land and negroes be sold and the proceeds be divided, and it for the appearing to the Court that William Rankin & Thos. A. Pope are responsible and discreet persons, that they are willing and qualified to make sale of the land and slaves specified in the complainants bill and that it is for the interest of the estate that they be appointed special Commissioners to see said land and slaves, wherefore it is ordered adjudged and decreed by the Court that said William Rankin & T. A. Pope be and they are hereby appointed special com. to sell said land and Slaves, that before they enter upon the discharge of said duties that they give bond with good Security payable to the State in the penalty of 20000 dollars.

Conditioned faithfully to perform said duties and pay over any moneys that may come to their hands by virtue of said Sale or Sales to the persons entitled to the same.

It is further decreed that Said commissioners after giving forty days written notice of the time and place of Sale at the towns of Pikeville Dunlap and Jasper as well as four other public places in the neighborhood of the land - proceed to Sell said negroes and said three tracts of land either in tracts or altogether as they may deem best, on the premises to the highest bidder on a credit of one and two years, taking note with good approved Security, for the payment of the purchase money, and retain a lien on Said land and negroes until said purchase money is paid, and make report to the next term of this Court, held after Said Sale takes place.

Ordered by the Court that James Heard be appointed overseer of a first class road from Coop's Creek to big Brush Creek and that he have the same bounds of hands as worked under former overseer.

P-115 It is ordered by the Court that John Ally be and is hereby appointed commissioner to examine and licens common school teachers for Sequatchee County for twelve months,-

There being no further business the Court adjourned until Court in Course
George W. Cain Churman
W. B. Elliott
F. M. McDonough

Dunlap Monday September 3rd 1860

County Court met pessuiant to adjournment - Present on the bench the worship chairman G. W. Cain and William B. Elliott and J. M. Morrison the following were the proceedings

Ordered by the Court that Wm B. Elliott and Jeremiah Walker Administrators of the astate of John F. Kennon Decast ask the further time tell the next term of the quarterly Court which was agreed upon and confermed by the Court.

James W. Hatfield Administrator of the astate of George Rogers Dec. made the settlement with the Clerk which was confurmed By the Court and ordered to be Recorded in the Book of inventories

Wm. Rankin
& others
vs
C. B. Rans &
others

Ordered by the Court that the decree obtained in the County Court of Sequatchee County By said Wm Rankin and others Be so changed as to allow the speshel commissioners in said cas to sell the negros specified in said decree on a credit of Twelve months P-116 in stid of one & Two years

The County Court aponted the fowling persons to act as Judges of an alection to Be held on Tusday after the first Monday in November nex for the purpis of Election Electors for President & vise president of the United States 1st District A. R. Thurman Thomas Minton & James D. Billingsley 2 dist. Louis Carlton J. C. Rickett and Jessa Savage 3rd District Wm Stewart Wm. Brown & Joseph Davis 4th District Wm B. Elliott Madison Deakins & George W. Cain 5th District John G. Barker John Hoodenpyl & Joshua Easterly 6th District Thomas Hicks Ephram Thurman & J. M. Morrison 7th District E. Newby Davis S.

Brown & David Varner 8th Dist. Charles Moffit E. S. Owings & I. N. Clark.

Court in Cours   Thare being no further Bisness Court adjourned until
George W. Cain chm
J. M. Morrison
W. B. Elliott

Dunlap Oct 1st 1860.

County Court met pursuant to adjournment present on the bench the worshipful chairman G. W. Cain C. L. Lewis M. B. Narramore W. B. Elliott F. M. McDonough W. E. Kell J. M. Morrison Simpson Brock E. S. Owins Byram Heard John C. Rickett A. J. Tate

The vote of the Court being taken on an allowance to Wm Johnson, of eleven dollars and seventy five cents for Services rendered by him as Sheriff of Sequatchee County which was voted in the affirmitive. (Iss'd)

W. R. Henson asks the Court to release him from his bond, in the case of William Hany being bound to him - which was aggreed P-117 upon by the Court and voted in the affirmitive.

The vote of the Court being taken on disanuling Thomas Pankey's Road leaving the Valley Road near Mary Stone's Barn crossing the dry creek above James Deakins so as to intersect the McMinville, and Chattanooga turnpike on the side Cum-berland Mountain which was voted in the affirmative.

State of Tennessee)
Sequatchee County)   We the special com. appointed by the County Court of said County to sell the land and slaves belonging to the Estate of Johathin Pope dec. after giving the notice required to be given by them proceeded to sell on the 29th dayof Sept. 1860. ad follows all the lands affirmed in one lott one track containing five hundred and ten acres described and shown by deed filed, one tract containing two hundred and fifty two acres adjoining the first tract as shown by deed and plot of survey, also one sixth partof a certain plot containing one hundred acres more or less adjoining the first named tract Thomas A. Pope, being the prucher at the sum of ten thousand dollars he being the highest and best bidder, Harv. was offered and cried off to Wm Rankin at the sum of one thousand and fifty dollars, he being the highest and best bidder Adison was offered and cried off to William Rankin at the sum of thirteen hundred and thirty dollars he being the highest and best bidder Charlotta, was offered and cried off to Benjiman Hawkins at the sum of eight hundred dollars he being the highest and best bidder, Ann was cried off to N. M. Pope at the sum of three hundred dollars he being the highest P-118 and best bidder, the above named land and negroes was offered and sold as directed by the decree. Notes and approved Sedurity hav bin taken - and a lean retained on

the land and negroes until the purches money is all paid, This the 1st day of October 1860.

       William Rankin
       Thomas A. Pope
       Special Commissioners.

 Ordered by the Court that Richard Jones be released from paying a poll tax for the year 1859 which is the tax for that year.

 Ordered by the Court that John H. Rogers, W. D. Stewart and W. R. Henson, be appointed commissioners on Edwin Newby's turnpike road.

 Ordered by the Court That William Rankin be allowed the prilage of makeing a small change on the cross Road near the Rankin Churchhouse provided that he mades the road so that the overseer and hands will receive it.

 The vote being Taken on an allowance of Two dollar and fifty cents to Each Justice of the peace viz Byram Heard A. J. Tate J. C. Rickett C. Lewis M. B. Narramore William B. Elliott F. M. McDonough William E. Kell J. M. Morriosn Simpson Brock E. S. Owings

 Elias McCarver presented into open Court the Scalp of a Wilde cat wich he proved to the satisfaction of the Court it is thare fore ordered that Certificate ishue

 Thare being no further Busness Court adjourned ontell Court in Cours.
       George W. Cain Churman
       W. B. Elliott
       Byram Heard
P-119 F. M. McDonough M. B. Narramore
   J. M. Morrison   C. L. Lewis
   J. C. Rickett   A. J. Tate

    Dunlap Monday Nov. 5th 1860

 County Court met persuant to adjournment presant on the bench the Worchipfill G. W. Cain Charman W. B. Elliott F. M. McDonough Byram Heard John C. Lockhart J. M. Morrison

 Wm B. Elliott and Jeremiah Walker admrs. of the estate of John F. Kennon decd having made settlement with the Clerk of this Court, which settlement being examined by the Court is in all things comfirmed, and ordered to be recorded.

 Ordered that John L. Smith be appointed overseer of a third class road in place of Elias McCarver and that he have the Same Boundry of hands as worked under former over-seaer.

 Ordered by the Court that Michael Miller be appointed overseer of a public road - in the place of John Picket, and that he have the Same bounds of hands as worked under former overseer.

Ordered by the Court that the Shiriff of Sequatchee County summon the following named persons good and careful men of Said County, to Serve as Jurors at the Decr. term of the Circuit Court for said County 1860.

Dist. 1st A. R. Thurman Byram Heard & Thomas Minton
" 2 Jesse Savage V. M. Lockhart Thomas Carlton
" 3 John H. Rogers Wm. Brown Wm. Stewart
" 4 J. R. Brown Wm B. Elliott Washington Cain & M. M. Phelps
" 5 J. C. Lockhart J. M. Anderson & Jones Mabry
" 6 James Deakins J. M. Morrison & Thomas Hicks
" 7 D. S. Brown Simpson Brock & John Picket
" 8 E. S. Owings Wm. McGlothlin Charles Moffatt

P-120 Dunlap 5th Nov. 1860

James D. Billingsley who has been appointed Deputy Sheriff for Sequatchee County appeared into Court and took the necessary oaths for his qualification

Warren Savage who has been taxed with a poll for the year 1860, appeared into Court and made oath that the time said tax was lexied he was over fifty years of age. It is therefore ordered by the Court that he be released from paying said tax and that the tax collector be credited with said poll.

Ordered by the Court that it adjourn until Court in Course
George W. Cain Cherman
W. B. Elliott
F. M. McDonough

Dunlap Monday Dec. 3rd 1860

County Court met persuant to adjournment present on the bench the worshipful charman G. W. Cain W. B. Elliott F. M. McDonough J. C. Lockhart J. M. Morrison.

Jessa Pickett presented a sworn certificate to the satisfaction of the Court that he killed one Wilde cat & Sckelp it in the County of Sequatchee in 1860. It is therefore ordered by the Court that Certificate isshue to him.

It is ordered by the Court that A. King be aponted overseaer of a public road in place James Seals and that he have the same bounds of hands as work under formed overseer.

Ordered by the Court that Thomas Carlton be appointed overseaer of a public road in place of V. W. Lockhart and that he have the same Bounns of hands as worked under former over seaer.

P-121 Dunlap, Monday, 3rd Decr. 1860.

William McGlothlin brought into Court the Scalp of one

PAGE 84 MISSING FROM MICROFILM AND FILE

PAGE 85 MISSING FROM MICROFILM AND FILE

Cat which he prooved to the Satisfaction of the Court was killed by him in Sequatchee County. It is therefore ordered by the Court that Certificate issue to him. (Iss'd)

It is ordered by the Court that Sarah F. Green have leave to move the remains of her father Alexander Green late of Marion County, from its place of interment to a Suitable burying ground.

Count adjourned until Court in Course.
George W. Cain Churman
F. M. McDonough
W. B. Elliott

Dunlap Tennessee July 6th 1863

No Court held in this period of time.

Dunlap Monday 14th day of August 1865.

The County Court for Sequatchee met and by proclamation at the Court house door, in the Town of Dunlap, and N. F. Burnett Esq. appointed Foreman by the Secretary of State untill Said Court be organized and they appoint their foreman. The foreman then adjourned the Court to meet on Tuesday morning 15th of August 1865 at 8 o'clock.

INDEX

Ables, David -88

Ables, Joseph -88

Abson, Joseph - 88, 191

Adams, Thomas -88

Adams, W. T. -88

Ahls, Benjiman -14, 45, 67

Ally, John -114

Anderson, J. M. -2, 77, 85, 91, 119

Anderson, John -61, 62

Arnett, Geo. W. -62

Austin, Elijah -10, 104

Austin, E. S. -45

Austin, Joel B. -24, 35, 36, 40, 42, 45, 50, 52, 53, 57, 64, 65
67

Bailey, B. J. -33, 45

Bailey, Benjiman -37

Bailey, Thos. -85, 107

Barber, James -7

Barker, Burrel -58, 93

Barker, Henry -38

Barker, Houston -59

Barker, Howell -2, 21, 38, 40, 67, 72, 73

Barker, John G. -5, 38, 71, 116

Barker, Moses E. -88

Barker, William -1, 2, 3, 5, 10, 11, 38, 39

Barnes, A. J. -71

Barnes, Charles, -72

Barnes, Thomas -71

Barnes, Wilson -88

Bennett, B. L. -5, 7, 10, 16, 29, 56, 71, 77, 91

Bennett, B. S. -89

Bennett, John -53

Bennett, John Sr. -9, 10

Bennett, Wm. M. -9, 10, 37, 95, 102, 103, 104, 108, 110

Bevert, Ausberry -32

Billingsly, James B. -37

Billingsly, James D. -116, 120

Billingsly, Joseph -10

Blain, James, 10, 17, 20, 35

Blair, James -13

Bowman, Andrew -69

Brimer, Aaron -44, 48, 56, 65, 71, 72, 90, 99

Brimer, A. G. -56

Brimer, Amos -56

Brimer, Wilson L. -56

Brock, Sampson -90

Bock, Simpson -37, 56, 60, 95, 99, 104, 105, 107, 108, 110, 111, 116, 118, 119

Brown, David -6, 59, 67, 72, 96, 116

Brown, D. C. -38

Brown, D. S. -119

Brown, Joseph R, 59, 63, 64, 77, 89, 105, 109, 111, 112, 113, 119

Brown, Lea -72

Brown, Peter -59, 75, 77, 103

Brown, Reuben -72

Brown, Rheuben -72

Brown, Sam M. -26

Brown, William -10, 45, 56, 67, 116, 119

Burg, S. J. A. -96

Cagle, Mrs. Barbary -86, 110

Cagle, Charles -70

Cagle, Eliza -86

Cagle, James -19

Cagle, John -35, 37, 41, 43, 48, 51, 53, 65, 66, 83

Cagle, Littleton -67, 85, 107

Cagle, Louise -96

Cain, Geo. W. -1, 4, 7, 8, 11, 12, 16, 17, 18, 21, 22, 23, 24, 25, 26, 28, 29, 30, 31, 34, 35, 36, 38, 39, 46, 50, 51, 53, 57, 64, 65, 69, 71, 74, 77, 79, 83, 84, 85, 87, 89, 90, 91, 93, 94, 95, 97, 98, 99, 101, 102, 103, 104, 105, 106, 107, 108, 109, 111, 112, 115, 116, 118, 119, 120, 121

Cain, Geo. W. Jr. -8, 41

Cain, John -13

Cain, J. S. -8, 9, 12

Cain, Esther A. -85

Cain, Washington -10, 45, 85, 107, 119

Camp, William -88

Cannon, Anderson -88

Cannon, B. B. -5, 10, 12, 13, 25, 28, 29, 32, 37, 43, 46, 56, 89, 92

Cannon, James H. -32

Cannon, John -5, 12, 32, 67

Caps, Melton -88

Card, Edward -72

Card, E. S. -9

Carlton, Lewis -10, 13, 68, 69, 78, 116

Carlton, Thomas -119, 120

Carlton, William -29, 70

Carmack, Elizabeth -58, 65, 89, 95

Case, Jacob -88

Cheek, Samuel -72

Childers, E. G. -72

Childers, Wesley -88

Christian, Peyton -20, 29, 88, 92

Clark, Bird -34, 44, 45, 85

Clark, I. N. -24, 25, 29, 34, 45, 36, 37, 40, 41, 43, 50, 51, 53, 59, 64, 65, 66, 67, 74, 77, 83, 84, 87, 90, 93, 103, 104, 108, 110, 116

Clark, Newton -5, 10, 20

Clemons, Elias -26

Clemons, James -6, 41, 71

Clemons, John -20, 32, 37, 66

Coleman, C. W. -13

Coleman, Washington -71, 72

Colms, S. H. -28

Connor, James -88

Conner, Wilson -88

Cope, James -76

Corêle Miligan - 6, 13, 19, 25, 37, 57, 66

Coulston, Jacob -72

Craig, Ake -14, 49

Davis, Alfred -53

Davis, Anderson -8

Davis Betsy Ann -19

Davis, Fountain -72

Davis, James -107

Davis, Joseph -12, 13, 19, 43, 45, 56, 116

Davis, Nancy -68, 69

David, Thomas -15, 45

Deakins, Franklin -1, 4, 5, 7, 8, 11, 12, 16, 17, 18, 22, 23, 24, 25, 30, 31, 33, 34, 35, 38, 39, 40, 42, 45, 50, 53, 57, 59, 63, 64, 65, 74, 75, 76, 77, 79, 81, 83, 84, 90, 91, 83, 94, 95, 97, 98, 108, 110, 111

Deakins, James -6, 108, 117, 119

Deakins, Madison -2, 5, 7, 10, 11, 29, 67, 94, 95, 96, 112, 103, 110, 116

Deakins, Margaret -90

Deakins, Mary -63

Deakins, M. E. -100

Deakins, Nathaniel -76

Deakins, Stephen -72

Deakins, William -6

Deakins, William R. -81

Dill, John -14

Dill, Overton -45, 48, 56, 91

Doooben, H. -60

Doolie, Harris -85

Dorris, W. D. -28

Dugan, Prudence -71

Dugan, William -45, 87, 88

Easterly, George -10, 19

Easterly, Joseph -7, 59

Easterly, Joshua -5, 11, 29, 48, 54, 55, 57, 67, 89, 105, 106, 116

Ellis, Mauzer -16, 19

Elliott, Wm. B. -19, 23, 24, 25, 26, 27, 30, 31, 33, 35, 36, 40, 45, 47, 50, 52, 53, 63, 64, 65, 66, 74, 77, 79, 83, 84, 85, 87, 88, 89, 90, 91, 93, 103, 104, 105, 106, 107, 108, 110, 111, 112, 115, 116, 118, 119, 120, 121

Ewton, A. B. -1, 3, 5, 10, 14, 17, 19, 21, 25, 29, 105, 109

Ewton, Caswell P. -32, 37, 45, 60, 85, 107, 110

Ewton, James -6, 32, 47, 71

Ewton, Sampson -72

Fairbanks, Levi -88

Farmer, James -57

Farner, James S. -71

Farmer, John -37

Farmer, N. -72

Fondrau, Samuel -88

Fredericks, Franklin -56

Fredericks, Isaac -56

Fredericks, John -54

Fredericks, William -93

Frizzelle, John -69

Gardenhire, El -71

Gray, Allen -67

Gray, Jehu -104

Grayson, Henry -5, 29

Green, Alexander -5, 121

Green, Sarah F. -121

Green, Thomas -88

Gilbreath, A. T. -37

Gott, Clabom -3, 16

Goulston, Joseph -9, 11, 42

Griffin, Howard -85

Griffith, Henrietta -65, 86, 96

Griffith, Howear -107

Griffith, John -34, 71

Hackworth, Austin -5, 89

Hackworth, Levi -31

Hall, Houston -88

Hany, William -116

Harmon, Bird -19

Harvey, Franklin -5, 7, 23

Harvey, Hezekiah -59, 93

Harvey jason -9, 10, 13, 15, 37

Harvey, William -5, 7, 23, 78, 79

Hatfield, Cornet-32

Hatfield, Eli -63

Hatfield, F. -107

Hatfield, F. M. -85

Hatfield, Gilbert -75, 89

Hatfield, Granville -21

Hatfield, James -21, 89

Hatfield, James W. -11, 12, 30, 32, 34, 59, 67, 80, 81, 90, 115

Hatfield, Jerry -89

Hatfield, J. H. -6, 8, 28, 69, 109

Hatfield, John -21, 76

Hatfield, John B. -11, 77

Hatfield, Jonathan -14, 17, 28, 30, 31, 32, 39, 86, 87, 90

Hatfield, Martha -21

Hatfield, Oliver M. -5, 7, 23, 58, 59, 98, 99, 103, 104

Hatfield, William -28, 84

Hawkins, Delila J. -112

Hawkins, Benjiman -112, 117

Heard, Betsy Ann -19

Heard, Byram -1, 4, 5, 7, 8, 11, 12, 16, 17, 18, 22, 23, 24, 25, 29, 30, 31, 33, 34, 35, 36, 38, 39, 40, 50, 53, 59, 60, 64, 65, 83, 84, 85, 87, 103, 104, 107, 108, 109, 110, 116, 118, 119

Heard, Geo. W. -29, 35, 37, 41

Heard, Harriet -70

Heard, James -61, 68, 69, 90, 115

Heard, John -45, 58, 61, 62

Heard, John Jr. -8, 14

Heard, John Sr. -19

Heard, Levander -61, 62

Heard, Martha -61, 62

Heard, Nancy -68, 69

Heard, Rebecca Jane -70

Heard, Susan -61, 62

Heard, William -5, 8, 9, 37, 97, 98

Heard, Williamson -88

Hendrix, Harvey -6, 31, 71

Henson, John -9, 61, 62, 78, 79, 90

Henson, William R. -61, 62, 69, 78, 79, 107, 116

Heron, John F. -59

Hicks, Isaac -29, 34, 52, 54, 55, 100

Hicks, James -19

Hicks, L. -40

Hicks-Thompson -1, 4, 5, 22, 24, 25, 35, 37, 53, 57, 64, 65,
    67, 74, 77, 116, 119

Hillis, Dixon -10, 13, 19

Hillis, Richard -44

Hixson, J. -28

Hixson, John M. -69

Hixson, Joseph -113

Hixson, Rubyn -51, 77

Hixson, William -13

Hoodenpyle, David -34, 49, 52

Hoodenpyle, John -48, 59, 64, 88, 116

Hoodenpyle, John W. -56

Hoodenpyle, Robert -85, 107

Hoodenpyle, Thos. J. -10, 67, 89, 107

Hoge, J. L. -10, 19, 40

Hoge, Joel -68

Hogem, J. W. -72

Hoots, Philip -5, 10, 32, 59, 60

Horn, John -69

Hoghes, Aaron -113

Hughes, John -90

Hunter, Malcom -42, 84

Jones, Elevin -47, 48, 50, 53, 65, 66, 74, 75, 86

Jones, F. M. -85

Jones, J. -69

Jones, James -12, 13, 59, 69, 89

Jones, Jospeh -86

Jones, Marion -9, 47

Jones, Martha Patience -21

Jones, Richard -118

Jones, Thos. A. -72

Jones, William M. -37

Johnson, F. J. -11, 30, 31, 32, 59, 90, 93, 94, 95, 97, 98, 100, 101, 102

Johnson, Frankin -76

Johnson, Isaac -38, 84, 85, 107

Johnson, Malcom -18, 85, 92

Johnson, Pleasant -37, 71, 76

Johnson, William -37, 57, 58, 67, 69, 70, 96, 97, 108, 109, 116

Kell, John -109

Kell, John Sr. -10, 59

Kell, Nimrod -11

Kell, William E. -10, 24, 25, 31, 34, 35, 36, 38, 40, 45, 50, 52, 53, 64, 65, 74, 77, 81, 83, 84, 85, 90, 93, 104, 107, 108, 110, 116, 118

Kennedy, Walter B. -59

Kennon, John F. -23, 27, 28, 115, 119

Kent, William -72

King, A. -120

King, Afred -19, 68

King, Andrew -71, 77

King, Thos. -37, 90

King, William -45

Lamb, Jo. A. -45, 69

Larrimore, Geo. K. -12

Lewis, Charles -47

Lewis, C. L. -92, 116, 118

Lewis, Jacob -103

Lewis, John -5, 9, 10, 12, 13, 59, 63

Lewis, Leonard -59

Lockheart, A. H. -24, 25, 30, 31, 37, 38, 43, 44, 46, 47, 49,
    51, 52, 68, 79, 80, 85

Lockheart, James -5, 8, 10, 14, 17, 49, 59, 67, 79, 85

Lockheart, John C. -24, 25, 30, 31, 35, 36, 37, 40, 48, 50, 52,
    53, 54, 55, 64, 65, 74, 75, 77, 83, 84, 85, 87, 88, 89, 90,
    91, 92, 93, 103, 104, 105, 106, 107, 108, 110, 111, 119, 120

Lockheart, N. M. -48

Lockheart, Robert -79

Lockheart, V. M. -71, 119

Lockheart, V. W. -120

Loven, Charlotte, -91

Lusk, Monroe -88

McBroom, Samuel -92, 97, 98, 100, 101, 102

McCarver, Elias -38, 72, 92, 118, 119

McClure, James -72

McDonough, Alexander -87

McDonough, F. M. -85, 95, 98, 99, 104, 105, 107, 108, 110, 111, 112, 115, 116, 118, 119, 120, 121

McDonough, Franes- 1, 4

McGlothlin, William -32, 37, 119, 121

McLain, Daniel -2, 7, 96

McLain, Elizabeth -2, 7, 96

McWilliams, Andrew 8

McWilliams, David -8

McWilliams, John -8, 23, 26, 69, 89, 104, 113

McWilliams, Riley -8, 84

Mabry, Jones -37, 67, 119

Mansfield, James -28, 41, 89, 100

Mansfield, Norman -86, 96

Mansfield, Rebecca -48, 75, 83, 86, 95, 96

Mansfield, Robert -71, 75, 83

Marlin, William -85

Marler, William -107

Mazy, John -72

Mickle, James C. -88

Miller, Michal -119

Minton, Joseph -59, 113

Minton, Thomas -5, 10, 29, 60, 89, 116, 119

Moffatt, Charles -44, 67, 85, 107, 116, 119

Morrison, J. C. -85

Morrison, J. M. -24, 25, 29, 30, 31, 34, 38, 40, 45, 48, 50, 52, 53, 65, 64, 67, 74, 77, 83, 84, 87, 89, 90, 93, 103, 104, 105, 106, 107, 108, 109, 110, 115, 116, 118, 119, 120

Narrimore, Frederick -45, 48, 50, 53, 36, 74, 83, 87

Narrimore, B. M. -24, 25, 26, 28, 30, 31, 34, 35, 36, 37, 38, 40, 42, 45, 46, 47, 48, 49, 50, 53, 57, 58, 59, 63, 64, 65, 66, 67, 68, 70, 71, 73, 74, 77, 79, 80, 81, 82, 83, 84, 85, 87, 89, 90, 93, 103, 104, 107, 108, 110, 116, 118, 119

Narrimore, Nancy -45, 50, 53, 65, 66, 87

Newbern, Aaron -60

Newby, Edwin -5, 15, 16, 18, 24, 27, 28, 29, 33, 34, 35, 36, 66, 74, 77, 83, 84, 87, 103, 104, 105, 116, 118

Nichols, A. J. -68

Nichols, G. W. -24, 25, 35, 36

Night, Dolphin -23

Odom, John -24, 30, 37, 40, 45, 50, 52, 53, 64, 65, 74, 77, 79, 88

Odom, William -72

O'Neal, William -20, 45, 71

Owings, Charles M. -91

Owings, E. S. -10, 13, 20, 24, 25, 29, 34, 35, 36, 39, 40, 45, 50, 52, 53, 59, 64, 65, 74, 77, 83, 84, 88, 90, 92, 93, 104, 116, 118, 119

Owings, John -91

Pankey, Thomas -6, 19, 27, 71, 108, 109, 117

Payne, William C. -61

Peacock, Henry -60

Perry, John -10, 45

Phelps, John -10

Phelps, M. M. -5, 6, 19, 29, 37, 47, 52, 53, 66, 68, 75, 76, 78, 83, 102, 103, 109, 119

Phelps, Mc -10

Phelps, William -16, 27, 59, 66, 75, 76

Pickett, Edward -34, 44, 109

Pickett, Jesse -2, 5, 14, 19, 25, 34, 44, 45, 54, 55, 67, 92, 100, 105, 106, 120

Pickett, John -7, 16, 34, 44, 54, 55, 56, 60, 64, 72, 90, 119

Pickett, John A.- 34

Pope, Byram L. -111, 112, 113

Pope, J. J. -28, 110, 112

Pope, Jonathan -5, 10, 26, 29, 32, 45, 62, 67, 95, 107, 108, 109, 112, 117

Pope, Leroy -112

Pope, L. M. T. -110, 111

Pope, N, M. -69, 110, 111, 112

Pope, Thomas A. -95, 107, 108, 110, 112, 113, 114, 117, 118

Porter, Mary Elizabeth -99

Porter, Washington -9, 10, 13, 59

Price, E. H. -86, 110

Priddy, Thomas -72

Privette, William C. -88

Ramsey, Champ -88

Ranes, C. B. -110, 112, 111, 115

Ranes, Mary A. -111, 112

Ranes, Mary B. -112

Rankin, Minerva -112

Rankin, P. F. -19

Rankin, P. S. -7

Rankin, Peter T. -104

Rankin, William -1, 2, 3, 4, 8, 16, 17, 18, 20, 21, 22, 24,
26, 27, 28, 41, 43, 46, 47, 49, 52, 59, 60, 62, 63, 64,
66, 67, 68, 71, 74, 75, 79, 80, 85, 89, 95, 97, 98, 105,
107, 108, 110, 112, 113, 114, 115, 117, 118

Reel, John -56

Reynolds, Robert, 71

Richards, James -3, 10

Richards, J. M. -18, 28, 40, 88

Rickett, I. C. -24

Rickett, John C. -13, 20, 24, 25, 37, 40, 45, 50, 52, 53, 64
65, 69, 74, 77, 83, 84, 85, 88, 93, 104, 107, 116, 118, 119

Roard, Eleven -72

Roark, Jerry -72

Roberson, Samuel W. -2, 5, 8, 9, 14, 13, 16, 18, 23, 27, 28, 29,
44, 50, 57, 64, 66, 71, 109

Rogers, Dauswell -84

Rogers, D. J. -91

Rogers, George -1, 4, 14, 30, 31, 34, 80, 81, 82, 115

Rogers, James I. -16, 51, 71, 77, 88

Rogers, Jo -54

Rogers, John I. -11, 16, 29, 43, 53, 56, 63, 64, 71, 89, 90, 91,
93, 118, 119

Rogers, Josiah -5, 30, 73, 81

Rogers, Patience -73, 80, 81, 82

Rogers, Roderick -60

Rogers, Susan -30, 80, 81

Rogers, William -12, 13, 18

Russell, John -10, 35, 44, 49

Samples, Charlie -98, 104

Saunders, Albert -67, 68, 89, 92

Savage Jessa -20, 23, 45, 67, 85, 89, 107, 116, 119

Savage, Warren -120

Sawyers, Eli T. -1, 4, 46, 100

Seals, James -77, 80, 120

Seatins, John -32

Simms, Thad -27

Simpson, Dr. John W. -28, 53, 59, 62

Smith, Aaron - 1, 4, 5, 8, 9, 10, 12, 13, 14, 18, 19, 22, 23, 24, 25, 29, 31, 33, 34, 35, 36, 38, 39, 40, 42, 45, 46, 47, 48, 49, 50, 51, 53, 57, 58, 59, 63, 64, 67, 68, 70, 71, 73, 74, 76, 79, 80, 81, 82, 83, 93, 95, 103, 108

Smith, Garrett -71

Smith, G. W. -32

Smith, Jackson -110

Smith, James B. -19, 20, 92

Smith, John L. -119

Smith, Susan -2

Smith, William -20, 72

Sparger, Harvey -69

Sparger, Samuel - 10

Stewart, George -10, 11, 30, 31, 32, 90, 100, 101, 102

Stewart, J. M. -66, 100, 101, 102

Stewart, William -37, 53, 65, 66, 83, 89, 116, 119

Stewart, William D. -1, 2, 3, 5, 6, 9, 10, 11, 12, 13, 15, 26,

William D. Stewart (cont) -29, 48, 57, 63, 64, 66, 71, 116

Stone, J. C. -43

Stone, John L. -1, 3, 5, 9, 10, 16, 29, 60, 61, 109

Stone, Mary -117

Stone, M. P. D. -59

Stone, S. 0. -1, 4, 16, 18, 24, 25, 27, 36, 54, 55, 66, 69, 73, 79, 84, 103, 109, 111

Sunns, Thos. -69

Tally, W. H. -45

Tate, A. J. -20, 23, 29, 43, 46, 47, 49, 50, 51, 52, 53, 59, 74, 77, 79, 83, 84, 85, 87, 89, 93, 103, 104, 108, 116, 118, 119

Tate, Jackson -67

Tate, James -71

Tate, J. W. -23, 33

Taylor, Burgess -1, 4, 10, 27, 29, 41, 53

Taylor, Robert -53

Teaters, John -19, 47, 60, 90

Terry, James -72

Thurman, A. R. -1, 3, 5, 8, 10, 37, 67, 85, 89, 107, 116, 119

Thurman, Ephraim -9, 10, 29, 53, 58, 65, 89, 116

Thurman, L. D. -31

Thurman, O. M. -37, 47

Thurman, Oliver -6

Thurman, S. D. -5, 7, 24, 35, 36, 37, 38, 40, 42, 45, 46, 47, 48, 49, 50, 53, 57, 58, 59, 63, 64, 67, 68, 70, 71, 73, 74, 80, 81, 82, 83, 84, 90, 93, 94, 95, 104, 108, 109, 110

Turner, Jonathan -56, 91

Turner, Joseph -45

Vandergriff, Jacob -60

Vandergriff, M. -60

Varner, David -45, 67, 85, 96, 107, 116

Vaught, Delila Jane -111, 112, 113

Vaught, Jonathan P. -111, 112, 113

Vaught, Leon Frank -111, 112, 113

Vaught, Leroy -111, 112, 113

Walker, Allen -85, 107

Walker, George -17, 19, 20, 22, 26, 27, 33, 43, 50, 53

Walker, George Sr. -71

Walker, Jefferson -59

Walker, Jeremiah -23, 115, 119

Walker, Philip A. -19, 22, 32, 39

Welch, Ephraim -5, 10, 23, 29, 104

Welch, John -2, 10, 45

Wheeler, Houston -10, 68

White -52, 61

Whitson, Bart -8

Williams -11, 90, 109

Williams, William -10, 25, 37, 41, 44, 50, 71

Wilson, William S. -88

Wimberly, J. C. -47, 100, 102, 103

Winchester, Joseph -60

Winder, John -56